LAURA SCANDIFFIO

THE STRUGGLE TO GO TO SCHOOL

 annick press
toronto + berkeley + vancouver

Edited by Catherine Marjoribanks
Designed by Kong Njo

Annick Press Ltd.

We acknowledge the support of the Canada Council for the Arts, the Ontario Arts Council, and the participation of the Government of Canada/la participation du gouvernement du Canada for our publishing activities.

ONTARIO ARTS COUNCIL
CONSEIL DES ARTS DE L'ONTARIO
an Ontario government agency
un organisme du gouvernement de l'Ontario

Cataloging in Publication

Scandiffio, Laura, author
     Fight to learn : the struggle to go to school / Laura Scandiffio.
Issued in print and electronic formats.
ISBN 978-1-55451-798-5 (hardcover).–ISBN 978-1-55451-797-8 (paperback).–
ISBN 978-1-55451-799-2 (epub).–ISBN 978-1-55451-800-5 (pdf)

     1. Education–Social aspects–Juvenile literature. 2. Right to education–Juvenile literature. I. Title.
LC191.S255 2016   j306.43   C2016-900226-8
                               C2016-900227-6

Published in the U.S.A. by Annick Press (U.S.) Ltd.
Distributed in Canada by University of Toronto Press.
Distributed in the U.S.A. by Publishers Group West.

Printed in China

Visit us at: www.annickpress.com

Also available in e-book format. Please visit www.annickpress.com/ebooks.html for more details. Or scan

To my children, Claire and Gregory,

who are embarked on

their own journeys of learning

Contents

Introduction

Have you ever been afraid to go to school? Maybe you hadn't studied for a test, or you weren't getting along with your friends. But what if you were afraid because just getting to school was full of danger? Or being seen in your school uniform made you a target for violence? Or if you knew that once you got there, you would be treated like an unwelcome outsider? And what if you knew that your family would go hungry every day you went to school instead of working?

Now imagine if someone told you that you could never go to school at all. Never learn to read and write or use simple math—what kind of future could you hope to have? Yet around the world, these are the challenges millions of children and teens face. For them, getting an education is a struggle against the odds.

Many obstacles might stand in the way of a child's dream of achieving an education. The stories that follow are true accounts of courageous young people taking on three of the biggest hurdles for children worldwide—poverty, discrimination, and violence. From Pakistani girls banned from school by the Taliban, to India's poorest child workers, to high school students in Chicago overcoming gang violence, these children face barriers that may seem insurmountable. And many have to battle more than one obstacle in order to learn. Yet there are amazing instances of remarkable young people overcoming these odds—and of teachers who are determined to reach the children who have been left out. Other inspiring young people have not only struggled to claim their own education, but have also become activists fighting for the rights of others.

Why fight so hard to learn? The people in these stories were motivated by the knowledge that education changes lives. They knew that children who get an education don't only grow up to earn a better living, they also understand their rights, improve their communities, and become the leaders of tomorrow. Education gives them control over their own futures, helping them to escape the traps of child labor, discrimination, and lifelong poverty. The people in these stories realized that an educated generation is one that can face society's problems head-on and help to solve them. For young people around the world, getting that education continues to be a struggle, but it is one they are determined to win.

POVERTY

"Everyone has the right to get education—and to give it."

— Babar Ali

Babar Ali decided to teach the children of his village who were too poor to go to school.

CHILD WORKERS

The Boy with a School in His Backyard

WEST BENGAL, INDIA, 2009

School was out for the day, but while the other boys lingered to play sports or hang around talking, Babar Ali rushed straight home. The tall, lanky teenager walked the first stretch at a brisk pace, the afternoon heat making him sweat under the white collar of his school uniform. Then he caught a ride on an auto-rickshaw the rest of the long way.

All day he had sat in the front row of his class, taking notes, his face frowning in concentration. And it wasn't just because he was studious. It was because he knew he would soon be passing on everything he had learned to others. He didn't want to forget a word.

Babar hadn't been home long before a brass bell rang loudly in his family's yard. It was 4:00 p.m. Suddenly children—dozens at first, then hundreds, of all ages—came streaming through the metal gate in the brick wall, many carrying books. The family's chickens scattered, then quickly settled back into their scratching and strutting. The kids' colorful clothes brightened the yard as they lined up in rows. Before them, Babar Ali, now in shorts, sandals, and a neat polo shirt, stepped up on a raised platform under a tree so all could see him. Together, they began singing India's national anthem, "Jana Gana Mana."

Soon the children were sitting cross-legged on the ground, their books propped open on their knees. Others were squeezed together on rough benches under a long, narrow shelter built alongside the yard wall. They would stay till the light faded, or till it poured, which happened often during monsoon season.

This was the only schooling these children had ever had. Babar Ali would teach them everything his teachers taught him, without asking for anything in return. For children with no other hope of going to school, it must have seemed too good to be true.

It Started as a Game

Babar Ali was very happy to be a student. Even though neither of his parents could read or write, his mother and father believed education was valuable and would change their son's life. And so Babar Ali was the first of his family to be sent to school.

The Raj Govinda school was run by the government, so it was free. The teachers there were well trained, and the classrooms had all the simple basics: desks, chairs, blackboard. Babar Ali had to pay only for his blue and white uniform and his books—about 1,800 rupees (about $28) a year. But in his West Bengal district of Murshidabad, many children were too poor to afford even that. Besides, they often had to work during school hours to earn money to help their families survive. The boys labored in fields herding livestock or cutting grass; the girls usually got jobs cleaning houses. Babar Ali knew he was one of the lucky ones. His father was a jute seller in Gangapur village. Babar Ali, his three siblings, and his parents lived in a

UNICEF, a humanitarian agency working for the rights of children, estimates that as many as 18 million children in India between the ages of 5 and 13 do not go to school. It is estimated that of the children who do start school, about 55 percent never finish primary school.

Why are so many children in India not getting an education? One important reason is that children from extremely poor families are often expected to work to contribute to the family income.

At first Babar Ali played at being teacher, but he soon realized that this was many children's only chance to get an education.

small thatched-roof house. By the standards of his village, they were far from poor.

When he was nine, Babar Ali came home from classes one day to find that some of his friends had stopped by his house. None of them could afford to go to school themselves. They were curious and asked him questions. What was a school like inside? What did he learn? Could he tell them? So Babar started a game in his backyard. He played teacher to his friends, repeating by heart everything he had heard during the day. He had a very good memory. And he discovered being the teacher was fun.

"My friends had never seen the inside of a school, so they enjoyed playing students," he explained. "They ended up learning arithmetic and enjoying it."

At first it was just for fun, but slowly Babar Ali began to see that the game could be turned into something much more valuable: "In the beginning I was just play-acting, teaching my friends. But then I realized these children will never learn to read and write if they don't have proper lessons."

Babar had always taken his responsibilities seriously. Now he felt strongly that it was up to him: the future of these young people was in his hands. And so, in October 2002, Babar Ali decided to make the game official. The grade 5 student opened his own daily school, outside in his family's yard. His students were eight friends who would come to learn after spending a long day working. What had started as a game was becoming a lot more real.

"Become big yourself, then help others"

Babar Ali's parents were impressed by their son's generosity. But not everyone was convinced the backyard school was a good idea. Some villagers grumbled, "What is the point of teaching children who should be working anyway? If you educate the girls, who will want to marry them?"

Babar's mother had mixed feelings at first. "Babar, focus on your own studies," she told him. "Become big and educated yourself, then help others to learn and grow."

But his answer was to remind her of the teachings of a Hindu spiritual leader who spoke of the importance of service to others. "Ma, haven't you read the works of Swami Vivekananda? So where is all this selfishness coming from?"

"I had to agree," she later said, "and inside I was happy my boy said such a thing."

Babar's father took a little more convincing. His dream was

Lessons took place outside in Babar's yard, where children as young as five sat on the ground for class.

that his son would get a job in India's civil service, where he would one day become an important man. But what was this now—his boy was running a school?

His parents wanted him to wait. "In all of India, run as many schools as you want," his father said. "But first fulfill my hopes for you."

But all around him, Babar could see children growing up without education, here and now. They could not wait. So neither could he.

"The way to a better life"

Word of Babar Ali's unusual school spread, and the number of curious children arriving at his gate each afternoon began to grow. Teaching so many children by himself, without books or classroom supplies, was going to be difficult. But Babar realized

Other volunteers joined Babar to help teach the growing number of children who flocked to his free school.

that there was another problem. Almost all these children were arriving hungry. How could they concentrate on lessons when their stomachs were empty? So Babar began providing them with a meal of rice from his father's fields.

Babar Ali's goals began to expand: teaching kids to read and write was an important beginning, but he wanted them to learn the whole curriculum of a regular school, including math, science, and Bengali, the main language of West Bengal. He knew he couldn't do this alone. One by one, he convinced students his age or a little older from Raj Govinda school to help out with the teaching.

Whenever someone asked why he was doing all this, Babar Ali would explain that it simply needed

"Without this school, many kids wouldn't get an education; they'd never even be literate."

– Babar Ali

to be done: "Our area is economically deprived. Without this school, many kids wouldn't get an education; they'd never even be literate." Again, he believed it was his responsibility, not just for them but for the society he lived in. "It's my duty to educate them, to help our country build a better future."

Babar Ali understood that education was the key to breaking out of a life of poverty. Like him, the new teachers knew they would be making an important difference. "Education dispels darkness. It's the way to a better life around here. That's why I come to teach," said Imtiaz Sheikh, a grade 10 student.

A local woman volunteered to ring the bell to call children to class.

In addition to the young teachers, another volunteer joined—Tulu Rani Hazra, a widow who earned her living as a fishmonger. Although illiterate herself, she became a valuable addition to the school. In the morning, as she sold fish from village to village, she also recruited new students, and she fearlessly confronted parents who had stopped sending their children to class. She found at least 80 new students for the school that way. Each afternoon she also proudly rang the brass bell to open classes.

Babar often turned to the Raj Govinda teachers for advice on his burgeoning school. With their recommendation and support, and that of sympathetic local monks, trust in the school spread. People who had once been suspicious began to donate money for books, pencils, and notepaper.

Local government officials heard people praise Babar's scheme, and they began to provide the midday meal and furnish books for the younger students. For everything else, Babar Ali and his students depended on donations from well-wishers.

Where No One Is Too Poor to Learn

What did a typical school day look like in Babar Ali's yard? At four o'clock, Tulu Rani rang her bell and the children streamed in, many carrying their own mats to lay over the muddy ground before they sat down. Another group of students sat under the shelter that lined one wall. Attendance was taken by the teachers, and each child was assigned a number to make this easier.

The youngest classes were the biggest, with grades 1 and 2 including over 200 students. Grade 8 might have as few as 20. The older students studied 10 subjects and were mostly taught by Babar himself and the volunteer college student.

The buzz of voices was constant as several classes went on at the same time. One young teacher, leaning forward in his plastic chair, was explaining the arithmetic of savings. On a low bench farther off, another described how energy acts on matter. In the shade of the makeshift shelter, a teacher quizzed her pupils on how an emperor used to get crowned. Whenever Babar Ali was not teaching, he acted as headmaster, strolling from group to group, asking how it was going and reminding his students to study hard.

Everyone worked on lessons till seven o'clock, when it began to get

"Education dispels darkness. It's the way to a better life around here."

— Imtiaz Sheikh, volunteer teacher

At one end of the yard, a shelter protected some of the students from rain.

dark. But because they were outdoors, a downpour could end classes abruptly. Some of the soaked students would run underneath the makeshift shelter, but the rest would dash home, slipping and sliding through the mud.

Changing Lives, One at a Time

It was very important to Babar Ali that his school be entirely free. He always found donors to pay for the children's books. No one was too poor to attend.

One girl at Babar Ali's school had worked every day since she was five, cleaning homes in her village. Along with her grandmother, she lived in a small thatched-roof hut with only a bed inside. Her father was disabled and couldn't work, so her family depended on her earnings, just 200 rupees (about $3) a month. After washing floors in one home and doing laundry in two others, she hurried each day to Babar Ali's yard and sat alongside the other girls on a bench. Sometimes she barely had time to finish work before class. But she looked forward to the time spent at lessons with her friends and dreamed of becoming a nurse. Before she found Babar Ali's school, it had never seemed possible.

"Here, we get books, rice, everything for free," she marveled. "Babar Ali's a very good headmaster. He doesn't ask for any money."

Although most of the students ranged from 5 to 14 years old, there were exceptions. One mother and daughter traveled far to learn together at Babar's school. "I couldn't help my daughter with her homework, so I decided to study," the 25-year-old mother explained.

"We are more like friends"

When Babar Ali turned 16, in 2009, his life was very different from that of other young people his age. Most boys he knew were students, or they were working to help their families. But by this time, Babar Ali had already been teaching after school for *seven years*. The number of children who came to his yard had grown to an astonishing 800. Many came only when they could, but on any given day, there might be close to 400 students squeezed into the yard. The youngest were four or five years old and the oldest were in grade 8. And they were still learning outside.

But now the school had a name. On a brick wall facing the gate, Babar had hung a sign that read, "Home of Joyful

Within a few years, hundreds of children were attending Babar's school.

Learning" ("Anand Siksha Niketan"). And he had more teachers! Ten volunteer teachers were pitching in, all students at high school or college. People asked him whether such young teachers could get the children to listen—after all, they were barely older than their students. Babar didn't see any problem. "The narrow age gap works to our advantage," he explained. "We are more like friends. The rod is spared in my school."

Maybe young teachers could still be effective, but what about a 16-year-old headmaster? Babar didn't worry about it; headmaster was not his most important role. "I feel I am a teacher first and a headmaster second. I teach my students with a lot of affection. Although they are different ages, they look at me as a friend and a mentor. This creates an atmosphere of joy and love and makes it easy for me and other fellow teachers to impart education."

And, of course, Babar was still a student as well, continuing to attend school during the day. He was excited about learning himself, and his enthusiasm got his students interested, too. "My favorite subject is history. I also like English and political science. In my school, I am the history and English teacher," he said. And as if that were not enough, he had bigger plans in mind. In addition to Bengali, math, and geography, he also wanted to introduce computers as a subject. Nothing seemed impossible now.

The World's Youngest Headmaster

There was no denying that literacy rates were climbing in the region thanks to Babar's backyard school. Local authorities began to recognize its value, and nine years after Babar held his first classes among the chickens in the yard, the school was registered with the West Bengal state government. This was very good news for Babar Ali's students, because it meant that when they had finished grade 8, they could transfer to local high schools and continue their education.

> "Everyone has the right to get education—and to give it."
>
> — Babar Ali

Babar found that at last he could reconcile his passion for teaching with his father's wishes. "At present I want to carry on teaching," he said,

Babar at his headmaster's desk

"but in the future I hope to join the civil service to help people in my society."

Babar Ali graduated from university with an honors degree in English, and he went on to pursue a master's degree in English literature. He has traveled around the world to speak about his school, and was invited to give a TED talk as "the world's youngest headmaster."

"We want the light of education to flow out from this school to the rest of the society," he has said. "Education for all. With that purpose, we have founded the school. Everyone has the right to get education—and to give it."

The backyard "Home of Joyful Learning" has continued to thrive and make a positive difference in Babar's community. Six of Babar's former students who graduated from the school are now teachers there—including his sister. The poverty that keeps millions of children in India from going to school is a complex issue the country is struggling to address. Advances have been made in getting more young children started at school; the challenge continues to be keeping them there, especially when poverty places them under pressure to work for survival. But individuals like Babar Ali have shown that it is possible to change the pattern, one life at a time, beginning with those closest to home.

Julia Bolton Holloway started an unusual school for Roma in Italy.

THE ROMA

Alphabets, Chisels, and Cradles: A Family School for Roma

Julia Bolton Holloway was walking in Florence, Italy, when she spotted a 10-year-old girl sleeping under the covered walkway of one of the city's beautiful Renaissance buildings. It was the Hospital of the Innocents, once a charitable home for orphans, and still used for children in care. Concerned,

Holloway searched for the director, and together they returned to discover not one but two girls huddled under ragged blankets. They took them for milk and sandwiches before bringing them to a local children's hospital. But the two girls escaped and disappeared within the day. All Holloway knew about them was their first names: Samantha and Marianne. They were two of the many Roma who live on the streets of Italian cities, begging for a living.

An abrupt change in Julia's life plans had brought her to Florence. Born in England, she had been for many years a respected professor and author, and spent her life teaching in American universities. But when she retired, she did something unexpected. She traveled to Italy and in 2000 became the custodian of the English Cemetery in Florence, a place where several famous English poets and writers are buried.

Julia's new work was taking care of the library and gardens and repairing the statuary. But soon she had a new idea: she would start a school. A cemetery seems like an unusual place to teach, but then, it would be a very unusual school. Julia's teaching would be tailored for the students she now had in mind: the poor Roma families of Florence.

Who Are the Roma?

The Roma (who in the past have also been called Gypsies) are members of an ethnic group that migrated from India to Europe between 600 and 1,000 years ago. Considered to be outsiders by the European communities they moved into, the Roma often encountered prejudice, and they protected themselves by creating a closed culture. Traditionally they lived in settlements that moved from place to place, as necessity dictated.

A Roma family in Suceava, Romania

ROMA REALITIES

According to a 2014 study by the World Bank,
"If you are a Roma child living in Romania
today, the likelihood that you were born into poverty
is three times higher than for other Romanians born
around you. You will likely grow up in an overcrowded
dwelling or a slum, and you will probably not finish
school, and you are not likely to find a job. Your life
expectancy is at least six years less than that of
your non-Roma peers."

Roma communities are now spread throughout Europe—especially Eastern European countries such as Bulgaria, Hungary, Romania, and Slovakia—and around the world. At about 6 to 8 million people, the Roma are Europe's largest ethnic minority.

They are also among Europe's poorest people. In Eastern Europe, 71 percent or more of Roma households live in deep poverty. Most families suffer from hunger daily.

Trapped in a Cycle of Poverty

Traditionally self-sufficient and mistrustful of mainstream European society, Roma families have often avoided schools altogether. And schools have not always been friendly places for Roma children. Many speak only Romany, and not the local language, so it's hard for them to fit in. They might start school later than other children and need to catch up. They are often targets for bullying by other students because they are poor and seem different. Roma children might be expected to stay out of school to earn money, often by begging. Unfortunately all this has made illiteracy common among the Roma.

In some places, Roma-only schools have been created to help solve the problem. But the students risk getting an inferior education at segregated schools. Either way, the number of Roma who drop out of school is high. In Romania, by the age of 16, only 29 percent of Roma boys and 18 percent of Roma girls are still in school. In a Croatian study, only 8 percent of Roma adults in Croatia had finished high school.

As a result, many Roma are trapped in a cycle: their poverty leads to little or no education, which in turn means no jobs and more poverty. As adults they can't afford to support their own children's learning, and the cycle continues.

A Different Kind of School

Julia Bolton Holloway puzzled over the problems the Roma in Florence faced. How could she help them break the old, vicious circle of poverty and illiteracy? Clearly what was needed was a new way to think about learning— one that would work specifically for this community.

One thing she understood was that any plan would have to include whole families. With the Roma, ideas were passed on not in books but verbally, from grandparent to parent, and parent to child, and skills were learned by hands-on practice. As Holloway observed, for the Roma, education was not accomplished "through being formally taught in alienating schools in rows at desks but through direct observation and practice within their families."

So if she wanted to succeed, she would first have to win over the parents. In many cases, she discovered, there was a lack of support at home for the child's school ambitions. Damian Le Bas, a Roma writer in England, explains, "While I went home to three generations of Romany Gypsy women who believed in literacy and read with me as often as they could, other families had different prior-

Holloway and one of her students prepare books for the Roma school.

ities, with some still believing that 'rithmetic' is the only 'R' that a Gypsy really needs in order to earn a living."

Roma women tend the flowers of the English Cemetery, home of the Alphabet School.

An Experiment Begins

Holloway's idea began to take shape. She would invite Roma families to meet once a week at the cemetery's library, where she and other volunteers would teach reading and writing. The approach would be practical, focusing on literacy and learning shared within the family. They would give each student 2 euros (a little over $2) to make up for the money they would have earned begging. And after class, students could earn even more if they liked, weeding or gardening in the cemetery, which had fallen into disrepair. Since literacy was the primary goal, the school was called simply the Alphabet School. As Holloway pointed out, "Accidentally I have discovered that if one has a garden . . . and a library, the two things [the Roman philosopher] Cicero said were needed for happiness, one has the ideal setting for education."

At first only Roma men came to the Alphabet School. Holloway was perplexed. Where were all the women and children? At last the men explained: Roma women refused to be in the same room as men who were not their husbands.

So that problem was easily solved. Two classrooms were set up. The men and older boys sat at a long table under an archway outside, while the women, girls, and young children met in the colorful, cluttered library. Gathered around a table like a family at dinner, the women and girls learned to read and write and were introduced to using computers. The younger children sat on the carpet beneath the bookshelves and browsed through the library's immense collection of illustrated books.

Learning was hands-on and got everyone involved. Together teachers and students created the picture dictionaries they would use, with words in Romany, Romanian, Italian, and English. The students made the drawings of people and things. One Roma couple began to write the schoolbooks together.

Holloway believed they were on the right track. She realized that during the early years of childhood, something crucial happened: children were set on the path of lifelong learning through school. But for Roma children, it was during these years that they traditionally learned skills passed on through generations from their families. She did not want them to lose one kind of learning to get the other: "Early learning is the most intense. It should not be at the cost of the centuries of skills which are lost when children

> "I have discovered that if one has a garden . . . and a library . . . one has the ideal setting for education."
>
> – Julia Bolton Holloway

Roma women and girls practice their writing in the English Cemetery's library.

As well as reading and writing, a young student learns how to chisel marble.

are taken away from their homes at the best age to absorb these in the family. I believe it is best to have schooling for the entire family, for it to be carried out in Romany, their language, in a library setting with books, where parents, grandparents, children, and grandchildren come together . . ."

In this way, the Alphabet School avoided a common pitfall. Sometimes when children go to school but their parents remain illiterate, it creates a gap between the generations. The parents might not understand the value of their children's schooling— or they might feel mistrustful about what goes on at the school. Holloway's "family schooling strategy" would instead add a new, shared culture to the Romany culture that was happening at home. She hoped this shared base would lay the groundwork for attending a regular school later.

Besides reading and writing, the students learned practical skills in the picturesque cemetery, its library, and workshop. Young men and women were taught how to chisel letters on marble or how to bind books. Together they built bookshelves and traditional wooden Roma cradles. Many Roma students took up the offer of earning money tending the cemetery's flowering gardens. Tourists arriving to see the famous cemetery would pass Roma students practicing their writing on outdoor tables, rocking babies, or gardening among the marble tombs. Within a few years, a crew of skilled Roma craftspeople were helping to restore the crumbling statues and ironwork throughout the cemetery. Slowly one couple saved enough money to build their own home in their native Romania.

Emir Selimi,
Roma activist
in Sweden

Taking Roma
Learning Online

Throughout Europe some remarkable people—Roma and non-Roma—have taken action to break the Roma cycle of poverty by providing education.

Emir Selimi had harsh memories of growing up in Serbia when it was part of Yugoslavia. He was kicked and spat at because of his Roma background, and he felt the pain of discrimination when he went to elementary school.

Emir moved with his family to Sweden when he was eight years old. In Sweden he found he didn't face the same old problems. But he never forgot his early school experiences. Knowing education was crucial, and that Roma kids often found it difficult to thrive in mainstream schools, he started a group called

Young Roma. The group created the first web-based Roma school, where students could learn online. Young Roma also strove to keep alive the Romany language, which had always been taught orally from generation to generation but was endangered in the modern world.

Emir Selimi traveled from school to school, talking to students about the challenges Roma face because of poverty and intolerance. He knew from firsthand experience that once Roma graduated from school, they faced prejudice from employers. To combat discrimination and ignorance, Emir offered to act as a liaison between Roma and the local authorities. His aim was to increase understanding between the 50,000 Roma in Sweden and the country's general population. In this spirit, he also made contact with Jewish and Muslim communities.

As Selimi saw it, learning about each other's cultures was the best way to end fear and prejudice. "In the end," he said, "when you get to know a person, you understand that they're much the same as everyone else."

In 2014, when Selimi was 31, he won the Raoul Wallenberg Prize—an award created to honor the Swedish diplomat who, during World War II, saved thousands of Hungarian Jews from the Holocaust by sheltering them or granting them Swedish passports. The jury that selected Selimi was impressed by his efforts to build bridges between the

"In the end, when you get to know a person, you understand that they're much the same as everyone else."

– Emir Selimi

often isolated and misunderstood Roma and Sweden's other communities.

"He is very much an inspiration, particularly for young people," the chairperson of the jury said. The prize included a much-needed donation to Young Roma and the online school.

Selimi said he was humbled to receive the award. "It feels fantastic; I can hardly express it in words what it means to us to be recognized like this in the spirit of Raoul Wallenberg—he was such a fantastic human being."

"I strongly believe that every person can make a difference," Selimi went on to say. "You don't have to be a superhero to stop racism or the injustices that can affect anyone."

"I strongly believe that every person can make a difference. You don't have to be a superhero to stop racism or the injustices that can affect anyone."

– Emir Selimi

Children play in a Roma settlement in Romania.

"Every Child in School"

As an American Peace Corps volunteer in Bacau, Romania, Leslie Hawke was deeply troubled by the sight of children begging on the streets. The ragged Roma boys and girls made a shocking contrast standing before the city's beautifully renovated medieval churches and soaring, modern, glass bank towers. The city of Bacau was a blend of old and new, with two universities and many scenic parks. And yet just past the outskirts was a settlement of one-room shacks on muddy ground that housed Bacau's Roma community. There, the people eked out a living taking day-labor jobs, foraging for scrap metal, and receiving small government payments. Modern technology and comforts were almost completely absent.

"There are these pockets of poverty hidden behind apartment buildings or on the edge of towns," Hawke explained. "There is little interaction between these Roma and the rest of Romanian society: educated Roma don't like to admit their ethnicity for fear of what people will think."

She began talking to some Roma mothers, who explained that no one wanted to hire them. One woman told her that she couldn't even get a job sweeping the streets. But the children could beg. While this might feed the family in the short term, Hawke realized, it also set up the child for a lifetime of illiteracy and poverty.

Hawke discovered that for every child on the street, there were two or three siblings at home in these shacks—and none of them was in school. Now she had a goal, and it was an ambitious one: by 2020, every child in Romania would go to school.

In 2006, Leslie Hawke teamed up with Maria Gheorghiu, a Romanian teacher. Their organization, called OvidiuRo, began training local teams in each community to recruit the poorest children for school. The mayor, local councils, principals, and teachers would all play a part. They would work together to find a way to change the school experience to make it work for Roma families.

Kindergarten Is the Key

Once they started working with Roma mothers and children, Hawke and Gheorghiu discovered that the Roma children who started school late—at age 8 or even as old as 12—almost always dropped out.

"If poor children aren't exposed to early learning opportunities, they never catch up to the other children," Gheorghiu

Roma children who start school early have the best chance of staying in school and graduating.

explained. But the earlier children started, the longer they stayed in school and the better they succeeded. So they had their first clue: kindergarten was the key!

In Castelu, Romania, the school principal called OvidiuRo for help. She knew that the poorest children in her area, mostly Roma, were not going to kindergarten. If they did start school later, they soon stopped coming regularly and disappeared altogether before grade 5. In August 2009, Gheorghiu arrived in Castelu to create a local action team. Volunteers knocked on doors in the poorest areas, asking parents to send their young children to kindergarten and their six-year-olds to grade 1. One volunteer walked through the village with a megaphone, announcing, "Education is free. We can help you obtain the necessary clothes and shoes and supplies." OvidiuRo's donors and the city's local council shared the cost.

So many children turned up that a new grade 1 class and teacher were needed. Space was a problem at first, and the grade 1 students had to take turns going to class in an old gas station across from the school. Most of the children thought it was fun.

The next trick was to keep the new students coming through the long winter. In the cold weather, many Roma became too discouraged to travel from their settlement to school, and they felt more pressure to spend their time foraging for food or begging to survive. Funded with donations, OvidiuRo gave parents food coupons if their children continued to attend every day. The results were outstanding. Hawke and Gheorghiu found that with this incentive and support, as many as 80 percent of the children kept showing up. To keep children on track, a daily after-school program offered homework help and snacks.

OvidiuRo's "Every Child in School" campaign, with its practical incentives and its goal of overcoming barriers, has been an encouraging success. And each success story that breaks this cycle also becomes a source of inspiration for other Roma children to follow.

Marijana Jasarevic, a Roma from Serbia and the first college graduate in her family, says, "We need more role models in our Roma communities to motivate Roma children not to

> "I try to be an inspiration for others . . . to encourage Roma kids and their parents to go to school, not to give up."
>
> — Marijana Jasarevic, Roma employee at the World Bank

give up on education, to inspire them with examples of people who made it from within our own communities. I would love to see more Roma teachers in both primary and secondary schools encourage Roma youth to believe in themselves." After graduating, Jasarevic tutored other Roma children. Later, working for the World Bank, she kept doing all she could to help young Roma: "I try to be an inspiration for others. When I have a chance to do field visits as part of my work, I always use the opportunity to encourage Roma kids and their parents to go to school, not to give up—giving up is a luxury, it is important to be persistent . . . I need to keep going and succeed."

Building Bridges

Thanks to the efforts of individual activists, there is an increasing awareness of what the Roma need to learn and thrive. In several European countries, governments have begun investing

After-school snacks are an important practical solution for Roma children, who often go hungry and drop out of school to help their families find enough food.

in programs to help include the Roma in society, especially through education. Emir Selimi approved of the Swedish government's pledge, beginning in 2016, to invest in training "bridge builders"—people who will work to increase understanding of Roma language and culture in and outside schools. However, Selimi points out that it's important that these efforts have the right focus. The goal should not only be integrating the Roma into European society but also increasing an understanding that goes both ways—with Europeans and Roma learning from each other.

That's a goal Julia Bolton Holloway has always understood and embraced. Some fifteen years after it started, her unusual Alphabet School experiment continues to be a success. While it may have educated a small number of Roma rather than thousands, the impact it had on those students was immensely positive. It also served as an inspiration for other homegrown, small-scale schools. Some of its students returned to Romania, where they began their own "alphabet schools."

Holloway acknowledged that she learned from her students just as they learned from her. "I have taught university students at Berkeley, Princeton, and Boulder," she said. "I prefer teaching illiterate Roma, all ages, and learning from them the richness of their culture, the excellence of their skills, and the strength of their families. We reciprocate, giving each what the other lacks, with dignity, in this pilot project."

DISCRIMINATION

"They say girls shouldn't get
an education. We say girls
will get an education
because it's our right."

— Shazia Ramzan

Malala Yousafzai

GENDER: GIRLS IN THE MUSLIM WORLD

The Other Malalas

In October 2012, 15-year-old Malala Yousafzai was shot as she rode the bus home from school in Pakistan. Her attacker was a member of the Taliban, a group that had targeted Malala for daring to campaign for the right of girls to go to school. Malala's father was an educator who supported his daughter's learning, and she attended the girls' school he had established.

Since the age of 11, Malala had felt the need to speak out against the Taliban's attempts to deny girls an education. In early 2009 Malala started writing a blog for the BBC using an assumed name, describing life under the Taliban. She appeared on television to talk about the need to protect girls' education in Pakistan. Soon her activism was well known, and she was even nominated for the International Children's Peace Prize. All this made her a target for Taliban militants.

Malala nearly died of the gunshot wound to her head, but after being rushed to a military hospital and later flown to Birmingham, England, for surgery, she astonishingly survived. And her story became famous. Continuing her studies in England, Malala also kept on speaking out for girls' right to an education, in Pakistan and around the world. In 2014 she became the youngest Nobel Prize winner in history when she won the Peace Prize. But, as she said, there are other "Malalas."

"I am not a lone voice. I am many. I am Malala, but I am also Shazia. I am Kainat."

She was recalling the millions of girls still unable to go to school in Pakistan and around the world—and in particular two friends who had been on the crowded bus with her that terrible day.

Shazia and Kainat

On the day Malala was shot, her schoolmates Shazia Ramzan and Kainat Riaz were sitting on benches in the canopied back of the Toyota truck that served as their school bus. They had just written an exam, and 16-year-old Kainat was talking it over with the girl next to her. Shazia, who was 14, stared at the passing scenery, daydreaming.

TALIBAN

From 2007 to 2009, the Taliban (a militant Islamic fundamentalist group) controlled Pakistan's Swat Valley, using intimidation and terror tactics to enforce their will on every aspect of life, including education. Girls, they believed, should not go to school.

Thousands of girls dropped out of school, fearing for their safety, and many schools closed for the same reason. Those that remained open were threatened by the Taliban, attacked, or bombed. At the height of their control, the Taliban had destroyed 400 schools.

In 2009 Pakistan's army forced the Taliban out and regained control, but the Taliban did not leave the valley altogether. Attacks continued against those who defied the Taliban's interpretation of Islamic law.

Kainat Riaz (left) and Shazia Ramzan (right), with their friend,
activist and Nobel Prize winner Malala Yousafzai

Suddenly the bus stopped. The girls in the back didn't know what was happening, but in fact a young man had stepped into the road and waved down the driver. He asked him, "Is this the Khushal School bus?"

As they were talking, another man climbed up on the open back of the truck. Kainat was too distracted to notice him. But Shazia heard him say, "Who is Malala?"

At these words, some of the girls glanced at Malala Yousafzai.

"He pulled out a gun and shot Malala in the head, and then shot me," Shazia recalled. "He started shooting randomly." Others remembered that his hand was shaking.

The bullets hit Shazia in the shoulder and hand. Kainat was shot in the arm. She fainted.

The bus driver rushed Malala and Shazia to a hospital. Kainat ran home, clutching her wounded arm. She had never been to a hospital and was too frightened to go without her parents. And she was still afraid of the attacker.

"I didn't realize his target was Malala, not me; I thought he will come again and he will shoot me," she explained. At first she believed that Malala had died, and that's what she told her parents when at last she staggered home.

Shazia needed surgery, and after that, she stayed in hospital for a month.

While Malala started a new life in England with her family, Shazia and Kainat remained in their hometown of Mingora, in Pakistan. Both girls discovered that although they had survived the brutal attack, their troubles were far from over.

When Everything Changed

Shazia and Kainat could remember how different things were in Mingora when they were little. Everything changed when the Taliban came. "Our school would open for one day and close for ten," Shazia recalled. "Nobody could concentrate on their education."

Shazia sometimes tuned her radio to the militant group's broadcasts. That way she could discover if it had declared a "no woman" day on the streets.

"They didn't want girls to get an education. They made it impossible for us to go to school. We couldn't even wear our school uniforms because

> "They didn't want girls to get an education . . . We couldn't even wear our school uniforms because that would identify us as students and put our lives in danger."
>
> — Shazia Ramzan

that would identify us as students and put our lives in danger. We were scared."

When the Pakistani army escalated its fight against the Taliban, both of the girls and their families had to abandon their homes to flee the scene of battle. When they returned, the town had been devastated by the fighting. "Everything was destroyed, but we were still happy to be home," Shazia said. "Although it was rubble, it was still our hometown."

The Next Target

The day after the attack on the school bus, fewer than half the girls in Malala's class showed up, but by the following Monday, only six were absent from school—a sign that many girls and their parents were refusing to give up. Shazia and Kainat were among those determined to keep going to school, but over time others became too frightened.

"Some girls are confident, but others look at how Malala sacrificed for her education and was attacked and they become scared and no longer want to study," Shazia explained at the time. "Some parents tell their daughters that what has happened to Malala can happen to them too, so don't seek education and don't go to school anymore."

Some neighbors wanted nothing to do with Shazia and Kainat or their families. No one wanted to attract the anger of the Taliban. In 2012 a bomb exploded near Kainat's house, terrifying the family and killing a neighbor. "Our neighbors said that I was the target, but that they missed and hit our neighbor's house," Kainat explained. They urged Kainat's family to leave the area. Kainat was in tears; she felt helpless. Leaving her home seemed impossible to her.

Both girls wanted to keep going to school—they both dreamed of becoming doctors—but just leaving the house felt more and more dangerous. The attack on Malala had become worldwide news, and Pakistani authorities feared Shazia and Kainat were likely targets for further Taliban violence. The army assigned soldiers to guard the two girls. Police vehicles followed the auto-rickshaw they now rode to school. Armed guards stood outside their houses and followed them wherever they went.

"I can tell you, my life completely changed after the incident, because before it, we could go freely wherever we liked on our own, but now we must be accompanied by guards who would tell us not to go out," said Shazia. "Even my parents would tell me my life is under threat. We'd want to go out and have fun but we were stopped. And we couldn't just go from school to a friend's place because our guards would come looking for us."

People survey the damage caused by a bomb blast near Kainat's home in Pakistan.

Kainat kept having nightmares about the shooting. But there was no question of giving up school, even if she and Shazia were scared.

"I have to be brave," Shazia said, "so everyone else can be, too."

A School in the Rubble

Like Shazia and Kainat, Parveen Begum could also remember when girls going to school was an ordinary everyday fact, before the rise of the Taliban. Parveen was the head teacher of Kanju Chowk Elementary School—a school for girls—in Pakistan's Swat Valley. Her school was once a busy, happy place. It had a reputation for excellence and was filled with many eager, ambitious young students. Then the threats began. Parveen was not fazed at first; she was not easily intimidated. But the threats escalated. By the end of 2008, the Taliban announced that all girls' schools in the Swat Valley would be shut down by mid-January.

"We were scared, but we stayed open."

– Parveen Begum

When yet another letter arrived at the school, Parveen knew what it would contain even before she opened it. She quickly scanned the contents, which confirmed her fears. It was another threat, the same as the others. If she didn't close her school, the Taliban would blow it up—with everyone in it.

"We were scared," she recalled, "but we stayed open."

In early 2009, soon after Parveen received the letter, a group of militants from the Taliban arrived suddenly at the school. Parveen steeled herself for the confrontation, aware of the many

Taliban threats prompted many girls to stay home from school; those who continued to attend class lived with the fear of another attack.

vulnerable young students nearby. She would have to keep from showing fear, and at the same time not provoke the men. To Parveen's surprise, they told her the school could stay open. But they had a condition. Everyone, even the youngest girls, would have to wear a burka, a long garment that covers a woman's or a girl's entire body and face. Relieved that they would be allowed to carry on, all the teachers and girls agreed to do as they were told.

Even so, within a couple of months, a Taliban bomb ripped the school apart in the night. The girls cried when they saw the classrooms reduced to rubble: walls blasted open, chairs and tables mangled in piles, and broken bricks strewn across the floor. Later that year, the Pakistani army won control of Swat Valley back from the Taliban, but everyone knew the militants still carried out attacks. Some were too afraid to go back to class.

Many destroyed schools remained closed, but Kanju Chowk reopened its doors within the year and welcomed the girls back. Parveen Begum defiantly began teaching again, in the midst of the rubble. She would show her students that a desire to learn could be stronger than fear.

Some girls were indeed too afraid to come back to class, or were forbidden to by their anxious families. But many of the girls bravely returned to classrooms that were now empty shells with dirt floors and crumbling walls—if the walls were still standing. Some classes had to be held outdoors. The youngest children sat in the courtyard surrounded by rubble, where they resumed learning the alphabet and repeating rhymes after the teacher.

"I was so upset. Our school used to be one of the best. But now we've fallen so far behind," said a 12-year-old girl.

"I feel bad that the Taliban don't want us to learn," an 11-year-old explained, "but we love coming to school. All of us here care about each other. The situation is so difficult, but the teachers are helping us."

Far from Home, Another Chance

After recovering from her injuries at a hospital in Birmingham, England, Malala Yousafzai and her family decided that she would continue her education at a high school there. So when an international boarding school in Wales offered her a full scholarship in 2013, she asked if perhaps the offer could be made to Shazia and Kainat instead.

The prospect of leaving home was frightening for the girls; neither of them had ever left Pakistan. But it would have been impossible to say no. It was a bewildering trip—each on her own—with only a little English to help on the journey. The highlight was a reunion with their friend Malala when they arrived in England.

When they first saw the boarding school that summer, Shazia and Kainat were astounded to find it was in a twelfth-century Welsh castle. Their new principal noticed that, despite their

PAKISTAN: AN EDUCATION CRISIS

Since 2010 it has been the constitutional right of all children to go to school in Pakistan, but in 2014 the country still had the second highest rate of children not being educated in the world.

Nearly half of Pakistan's children are not in school. And the situation is worse for the country's girls. Alif Ailaan (a campaign for education reform in Pakistan) estimates that 55 percent of all school-age Pakistani girls do not get an education—about 13.7 million girls. The most common reason given is that their parents do not allow it. In many rural areas, it is not yet the social and cultural norm for girls to go to school.

ordeal, the girls were resilient and delighted to experience new things. Although Kainat still suffered from nightmares, and the new surroundings were strange, she was determined to make the most of the extraordinary opportunity she had been given. Shazia felt the same way: "I was a common girl from Swat Valley . . . I've come so far. My parents could not afford it . . . I have so much freedom, unlike in Swat. I can do whatever I want here." And for the first time in ages, she felt safe.

The girls' teacher was impressed that within their first year of learning English, they were willing to try public speaking. They drafted speeches to tell their story to their classmates, and then read them again at a Rotary Club conference. Although older, Kainat was shyer about speaking than talkative Shazia, but she kept at it.

"They know that the issues are, for them, far more important than themselves," their teacher said. "They're not egotistical kids who want to be in the limelight—they're very humble girls."

"If we speak up, other people will follow us"

Both Shazia and Kainat stuck to their longtime dream of becoming doctors, and they intend to return home once they have earned their degrees. "I think this is the very best way for us to help other people," Kainat explained. "I want to become a gynaecologist, because in our society there are lots of male doctors, but not female doctors, and in our religion the women can't show their bodies to men.

"But I also want to join other charity groups, especially focusing on girls' and boys' education. For me, education is like light—without light you can't see anything."

"Don't worry," Kainat had told her anxious father before leaving for England. "One day I will be successful and then I will come back to Pakistan."

Shazia also believes that finishing her education will give her an opportunity to do something for girls back home. "I will complete my studies so I will go back and help these people and help these girls," she said. Their friend Malala continues to be a hero and inspiration for both of them.

"Our fight is for education," Shazia told an interviewer before leaving Pakistan. "They say girls shouldn't get an education. We say girls will get an education because it's our right.

"If it had said in Islam that we shouldn't be educated, then our parents would have stopped us. But our parents support us and tell us that whatever our ambition is, we should achieve it. So this is the thing everybody—everybody—should fight for, because it was through education that man walked on the moon."

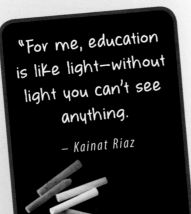

"For me, education is like light—without light you can't see anything.

– Kainat Riaz

Kainat has tried to view their nightmarish experience as one step toward a greater goal. "Before we were shot, there was hardly any concept of sending girls in Swat to schools, but now parents have started to do that," she said.

Despite opposition from extremists, education for girls is indeed slowly on the rise in Pakistan and Middle Eastern countries. Although in many areas girls must still overcome the long-held attitude that they do not belong in school, there is a growing awareness that literate, educated girls and women

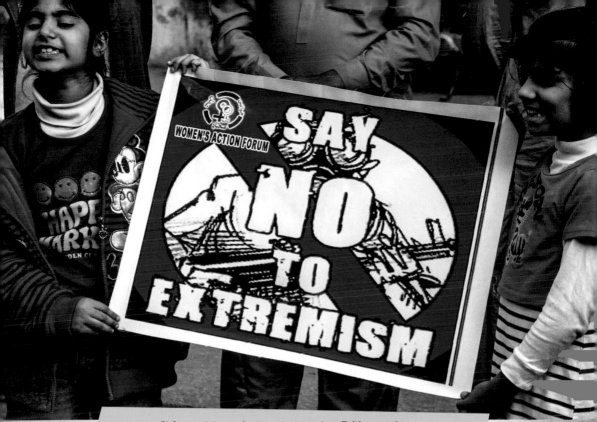

Girls participate in a protest against Taliban violence.

benefit everyone—from their families to society as a whole. But it is a struggle for equality that is ongoing. Like Kainat, Shazia has also realized that their actions and words now can make a big difference to the future of this struggle: "I think if we speak up, then other people will follow us."

"So this is the thing everybody—everybody—should fight for, because it was through education that man walked on the moon."

— Shazia Ramzan

Karachi, Pakistan, where Maria Taqdees lived after her arranged marriage

Sharing the Knowledge that Changes Lives

Fifteen-year-old Maria Taqdees was happy to be going home. She had left Pakistan in 2004 to spend a year in the United States as an exchange student in a Nevada high school.

"That year was living my dream, learning so much in school," she said. And now she was returning home, brimming with confidence from her year away and all her recent experiences. She was eager to finish high school in her own country and to put into practice everything she had learned.

Her family, however, had other plans for her. As was the custom for many teenage girls in her community, a marriage had been arranged for her. And just like that, her plans for further schooling came to an abrupt halt.

Maria was soon married and went to live with her new husband in Baldia Town, an impoverished area of Karachi, Pakistan. Her husband's family was poor; his father was a rickshaw driver. In fact, most of the working people in Baldia Town drove rickshaws, trucks, or taxis, or else worked as daily laborers. Many could not read or write.

The move was a shock to Maria. Most of the young girls in the neighborhood didn't go to school because their parents could not afford it. The local people were conservative in their attitudes and beliefs, and women were discouraged from leaving their homes. Most mothers were illiterate.

"I was miserable," Maria recalled. "I couldn't believe that I was an educated girl; I knew English . . . and all the girls and women around me were almost illiterate. There was no access to computers and to the world. I did not fit in."

Starting from Scratch

Three years passed as Maria tried to feel at home in her new life, without much success. But then she began to look at her situation the other way around.

"I realized I was educated; I was fluent in English . . . And although I did not get a chance to finish high school, I could teach something to these girls around me.

"I decided that instead of staying depressed and cursing my situation, I would help women in my community gain an education and hopefully help them better their lives."

Maria had witnessed firsthand how a lack of education made life difficult for these women in so many ways. They couldn't

Girls learn computer skills in Maria's classes.

do simple arithmetic when they were shopping for the family's meals. They couldn't take a public bus anywhere because they couldn't read the signs. They didn't know how to use a cell phone. She also saw that when mothers couldn't read, they couldn't help their children learn. Now she saw a way she could make things better.

"Although I did not get a chance to finish high school, I could teach something to these girls around me."

— Maria Taqdees

Maria asked her husband, who worked for the navy, to help her find a computer to get started on her project. To raise money, she sold her wedding ring. And she set up a class in her own bedroom. "My humble one-bedroom home became a community learning center during the daytime," she explained.

Soon she had two donated computers. And her experience in America came in handy, too. "To create the curriculum, I used all the resources I had from my high school in the U.S.," she said. "I had brought everything back with me."

At first she got little encouragement from her community: "The girls' families and even local religious leaders first doubted my intentions." But Maria persevered. She knew she would have to be patient and build their trust.

Maria started with simple goals. She wanted to give the girls and young women a chance to learn English and computer skills. With the older women she invited, Maria would focus on basic literacy for daily needs. "They wanted practical education, such as being able to read the signs on the bus or the roads."

A few girls were willing to try the classes. Some were already in school, and some had gone to school and stopped. Even so, Maria found they had not learned very much. With Maria, they studied English for two hours a day, five days a week. And the computer training was practical, too. The girls learned how to use the Internet and all the technical terms they needed to understand it.

After three months, most of the girls were proficient on the computer, and many of her older students could read and understand newspaper stories, signs, and bus routes. The classes also became a place for lively discussions among the women, who often felt very isolated at home. Their confidence grew.

Some of Maria's students wanted to become doctors, but at the same time, many just needed skills to earn money and support their families. One girl, whose father collected and sold junk on a cart, completed the computer-training program. Soon afterward, she got a job that paid enough for her to cover the cost of her family's housing and her siblings' education. A few of Maria's students became teachers in neighborhood schools. Maria was encouraged by each success. She knew she had found what she wanted to do with her life.

Achieving Their Dreams

Maria's students learn practical skills such as sewing to earn an income.

As she spent more time with these girls and women, Maria learned about the obstacles they faced. Some of them had dreamed of continuing on to higher education, but they never got the chance. In many other cases, their husbands objected to women working outside the home, and yet the family was barely surviving on a dollar a day.

"I started to realize that the women needed other skills to progress," Maria said. She wanted to offer them a kind of training that would allow them to work at home and boost the family's income. So Maria brought in other women volunteers to teach practical skills, such as sewing and handicrafts. In 2014 she got in touch with an organization called YES (Youth Exchange and Study), the same organization that had funded her year in the United States. They helped Maria by giving her a small grant to set up her vocational training program.

Handicrafts such as these were offered for sale by Maria's students.

Many local girls enrolled to learn from the skilled artisans. Soon Maria's students had produced an impressive array of clothing, handbags, and jewelry. The bedroom and the rest of Maria's house were now overflowing with students, teachers, and their creations. They would soon need a bigger space!

Maria next wanted to help the women display and sell their work. She held an exhibition at a local hotel, and it was successful enough that she began planning larger exhibitions. She hoped that with their new English and computer skills, the women could even reach a global market by running an online business from home.

Meanwhile other volunteers joined her cause, young students who wanted to share their education as well. Maria kept up the school, even as she became a mother herself. In fact, she found that her children inspired her. Her husband came to

Maria Taqdees talks about her successful home-based school in the hope of spreading the idea to other communities in Pakistan.

believe in her school and lent his support, too. "My husband is my best friend," Maria said. "He has supported me all these years, even when he did not understand what I was trying to do."

By 2015 over 200 women and girls had graduated with the certificate Maria created for her program. As the school grew, so did Maria's vision. She next wanted to expand the idea to other cities in Pakistan.

"In all of these places, there are women and girls in need of basic educational and vocational skills that will allow them to work toward achieving their dreams," Maria explained. "My hope is to continue to be part of that education process."

India's Mushahar girls belong to a group traditionally called "untouchable."

CASTE

Outcasts from Learning: Teaching the Untouchables

BIHAR, INDIA

A young girl just starting school walked into her classroom for the first time. Shy among the strangers and used to keeping a low profile, she sat quietly on a bench at the back.

She was very careful not to bother anyone or draw attention to herself, but when the other children arrived, they ordered her off the bench, and she obediently moved to sit on the floor.

As the days passed, her classmates were careful not to let her touch any of their belongings, not even a piece of paper or a pencil. If she asked them to pass a book to her, they would refuse.

School is not easy for anyone who feels like an outsider. But for the children of India's Mushahar—the "rat eaters"—it could be unimaginably difficult. And for a Mushahar girl, it was nearly impossible.

The young girl belonged to the lowliest group in her society, outsiders who had for centuries been called "untouchable."

"To love those who have never been loved"

In 1964, a teenage girl sat in a different classroom, completely absorbed in a magazine she had found there. She was not Mushahar—far from it. Her family was comfortably well-off and owned a plantation in the south of India, in the state of Kerala. Sudha Varghese had never even seen a Mushahar slum or village. But she was engrossed by the stories in her magazine about nuns and priests who worked with the poor in Bihar, one of India's most impoverished states, far in the north.

Sudha was shocked by descriptions of people who had nowhere to sleep at night. She knew the workers on her family's land were poorer than she was, but they earned a reasonable wage, and she had always played with their children after school. This was completely different.

"I first heard of Bihar when I was in class tenth," she recalled later. "And I was touched even by the secondhand description of the homeless, hungry, and . . . hopeless people."

INDIA'S UNTOUCHABLES

Traditionally India's Hindu society was divided into groups, known as castes. A person's caste was determined by his or her family and job, and people generally did not mix with or marry people from another caste. Castes were ranked in a hierarchy from highest to lowest.

At the very bottom of this ranking were people who did menial jobs that higher castes considered beneath them, because such tasks "polluted" the worker. For this reason, such people were considered untouchable by those in the higher castes, who would not touch or even be near them.

In 1949 India's new constitution outlawed discrimination based on caste. The people once called untouchables now began to call themselves "Dalits," which means "crushed" or "oppressed." But while caste discrimination is no longer legal, it is still a fact of life in parts of India, especially outside the cities in rural villages. The northern states of Uttar Pradesh and Bihar are home to the poorest of the Dalits. They are often called "Mushahar," which means "rat eaters."

Today there are around 170 million Dalits in India, about a sixth of the population. There are about 2 million Mushahar in and outside Bihar.

Even when Dalit children are fortunate enough to attend school, they must overcome discrimination based on their caste.

Soon afterward, a group of nuns, the Sisters of Notre Dame, visited Sudha's town. The nuns ran a school in Bihar for the poor, and they were looking for people willing to come join them there, to help those less fortunate and "to love those who have never been loved."

The call for help sparked something in Sudha, and her response was impulsive and stubbornly decisive. She didn't even think twice. She would go.

Her family was shocked. How could they even consider letting her go? The faraway state of Bihar was like a "foreign land" to them, and they knew life would not be easy for Sudha there. But Sudha would not let them talk her out of it—her mind was made up and nothing would change it. And so, at last, they reluctantly gave their permission.

After a four-day train journey, 16-year-old Sudha arrived in Bihar in India's faraway northwest. She finished her schooling there, and after graduating became a nun, joining the Sisters of Notre Dame and teaching in their schools.

Sudha was happy to be teaching and making a difference, but still, the experience wasn't exactly what she had expected. The schools were in the city, and she still felt too far from those who needed help the most. She would have to strike out on her own—out to the far-flung villages of the country-side—to find the people she really wanted to help.

> "I wanted to be with the poor—and not just the poor, but the very poorest among them. So I went to the Mushahar."
>
> – Sudha Varghese

In her words, "I wanted to be with the poor—and not just the poor, but the very poorest among them. So I went to the Mushahar."

Moving in with the Mushahar

Sudha's next decision shocked many people—she wanted to go *live* in a Mushahar village. "People from other castes and communities despised me," she said, but she paid no attention. "It was a small beginning for me."

Sudha had a good idea of what to expect—she had braced herself for the abject poverty she knew she would find among the Mushahar—but she was still horrified by what she saw when she arrived at the village. The muddy lanes between squalid huts were littered with animal waste and garbage, and crawling with flies. There were no latrines and nowhere to wash. Forcing

Houses in a Mushahar village

herself to see past the squalor, she asked the villagers if she could stay. They were amazed. Sudha shared a one-room shack with a family.

The poorest of the Dalits, the Mushahar worked mostly as farm laborers for a pittance in wages. Very rarely did the Mushahar own land of their own. Only about two in every one hundred Mushahar men could read—and fewer than one in a hundred women. They lived apart from the rest of the population, shunned and avoided.

In Sudha's words, "They are the most vulnerable, the most marginalized, and the poorest of the poor in every sense." And

"They are the most vulnerable, the most marginalized, and the poorest of the poor in every sense."

– Sudha Varghese

the least-valued person within this despised group was a girl Mushahar, often reduced to eating scraps when all the men and boys were done. It was toward these girls that Sudha turned her attention.

She watched a tiny little girl, wearing nothing but torn underpants, who was waving a stick to herd pigs. In the evening Sudha borrowed the girl's stick and began to draw letters in the dirt on the ground. In this way, she taught the little girl—and the other children—the alphabet.

Sudha talked to their mothers, too, about their health, and raising children, and how hygiene could keep them from getting sick. Even though she was a nun, she saw her mission among the Mushahar as humanitarian, not religious. She called herself a social activist.

"Wherever I see there is something lacking in [their] being a fully human being," she explained, "I like to support them and see that they reach their full human good—that is my purpose."

The Cycle Sister

Sudha called her project among the Mushahar Nari Gunjan, which means "women's voice." With donations from her family and a little from the local community, she set up an educational center for Mushahar girls. At the center they could learn basics like reading and math—and, importantly, skills that could earn them an income, from sewing to bedside nursing. They also learned about their health and their legal rights.

Sudha knew many of these girls would be married by age 12 or 13, as was the custom. They might have several children by the time they were 30. She realized that the one important role Mushahar girls had was as mothers in charge of

Sudha Varghese teaching Mushahar girls to read and write.

their households. In this way, they had an impact on everyone's life. By teaching them now, she could help them change their community for the better when they grew up.

It dawned on Sudha that educating the girls was the key to a better future for all the Mushahar. "Unless the girls become strong, educated, and aware, this community will never change," she realized.

"Unless the girls become strong, educated, and aware, this community will never change."

— Sudha Varghese

Sudha wanted to start more education centers across Bihar so that she could help more Mushahar, and with a grant from UNICEF, she was able to make that happen. Now she rode her bicycle from one center to another, supervising them all. With her long hair pulled back in a braid and dressed in a simple sari with a bag slung across her body, the energetic nun became a familiar sight pedaling from village to village. Locals started calling her the "cycle sister."

Soon Nari Gunjan included 50 educational centers for Mushahar girls, helping around 1,500 students. While Sudha was teaching all these girls, she also encouraged them and their parents to peacefully stand up for themselves. Ignorant of the law and their rights, Mushahar were often cheated. Once, when

Sudha receives an award in 2006 from the president of India for her devotion to helping the Mushahar.

Mushahar laborers had worked all day, the landowner who had hired them refused to pay their wages. Sudha led them to sit peaceably on his land and not move till he paid them what they were owed.

Now her next step seemed clear. In order to help fight for the rights of the Mushahar, Sudha would become a lawyer! Sudha decided to go to law school, and she earned her law degree in 2000, when she was 50. After that, she often appeared in court, fighting cases for Dalits.

Sudha Varghese lived with the Mushahar for 21 years. In the end, she explained, she simply "became Mushahar."

"Inspiration": A Home and a School

The education centers were a big step forward, but Sudha knew that it still wasn't enough. The centers offered basic knowledge and valuable skills, but they did not replace formal schooling and diplomas. Mushahar girls were unwelcome in most village schools, and even if they did go, they were almost never able to study enough at home to succeed. Hand-pumping water, herding animals, scouring pots, and preparing food— their chores never ended.

"They will never find even half an hour to get back to their books when they are at home," Sudha explained. "They'll always be working."

What they really needed to succeed was to get away—to have a place to stay where they would be welcome, fed regular meals, and able to concentrate on learning.

In the town of Danapur, not far from the city of Patna, Sudha found a rundown building. Volunteers helped to make it livable, with money from donors and help from the state government.

Girls who have come to learn at Prerna embark on a new life.

She called the new hostel and school Prerna, which means "inspiration" in Hindi. Now, how to convince the families to let the girls leave home? It was very unusual for a young, unmarried girl to live away from her family, but Sudha was persuasive. Her first students arrived in 2006.

The little girls were unused to schedules, classes, or daily baths. Many found the new school a bit overwhelming, and they would look at the ground, avoiding their teachers' eyes. Sudha found that they struggled to concentrate on a subject for even half an hour. They were dreamy and easily distracted. But regular meals helped improve that, giving them energy to focus. Bihar's government paid for the meals at Prerna through one of its social programs to improve life for the Dalits. Many girls had never seen so much food in their lives: naan bread and rice and dahl. And they were allowed to fill their plates!

"Take only what you need," Sudha reminded them.

A Different World

Life at school was very different for the girls in other ways, too. At home they were used to being the least important, almost unwanted. As Sudha explained, "All that they have known and heard and seen is, 'You are like dirt.' They have internalized this: 'This is my lot' they feel. 'This is where I belong. I don't belong on the chair. I will sit on the floor, and then no one can tell me to go any lower than that.'

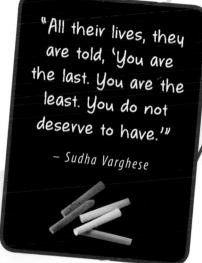

"All their lives, they are told, 'You are the last. You are the least. You do not deserve to have.'"

– Sudha Varghese

"All their lives, they are told, 'You are the last. You are the least. You do not deserve to have.' They learn very fast to keep quiet, don't expect changes and don't ask for more."

But Prerna School was like another world. The girls played sports, raised their voices, and laughed out loud, unafraid that anyone would shame them for being seen or heard.

Well fed for the first time, many girls had growth spurts during their first few months at school. Sudha had to warn their parents not to pull the girls out of school for early marriage—a common practice—just because they looked so much taller. That would end everything they had worked for. She warned the mothers of new students right away: "In five or six years they will start looking big. Then don't start thinking they have grown up and we have to get them married . . . When you look all around you, you see that educated people have more opportunities."

Sudha raised money to send the most promising students to a nearby private school during the day. She found unemployed university graduates as teachers for the rest. They taught India's standard curriculum, plus singing, painting, and computers. In the early days they also taught the young girls basic things like how to clean themselves properly and how to care for their health.

Sudha encouraged the girls to study hard and always lavished praise on them for their accomplishments, even little ones. More was at stake here than learning facts: she wanted to see their self-respect grow and see them start to have dreams for a bright future. Perhaps most important of all, Sudha wanted them to be able to believe that they deserved that future.

"Power to take charge of their own lives"

With all this in mind, Sudha decided to add one more surprising subject: karate.

"Right from the beginning, I wanted to give them karate because one of the things they lack is self-confidence," she explained. Sudha also hoped it would offer these vulnerable girls some self-protection. "With karate, we tried to give them a sense of power to take charge of their own lives."

It turned out to be a brilliant idea. In 2011, 20 of the girls took part in a national karate competition. It was the first time they had gone anywhere other than their village or Prerna. They returned with five gold and five silver medals, and they were even invited to the Asian championships in Japan. The girls

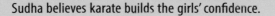

Sudha believes karate builds the girls' confidence.

were amazed by the urban landscape of skyscrapers, and by the respect they were shown. Later they traveled to Armenia for an international championship.

With their new self-confidence, the girls aspired to more than medals. One of Prerna's karate champions, who came from a Mushahar slum in Patna, set a new goal for herself: to someday be a judge.

By 2011 there were 125 girls at Prerna. Several, resisting the pitfalls of early marriage or return to work, had already graduated from high school. One special young woman who had made it all the way to graduation was Sudha's first student, the very same little girl whose stick Sudha had borrowed to teach the alphabet all those years ago. Sudha had convinced her

Mushahar girls, with the knowledge and self-confidence they've gained from Prerna, are ready to face life's challenges.

reluctant parents to send her to Prerna. Now she was educated and in her twenties, and, like many of her friends, thinking of marriage.

Sudha was determined that if her earliest pupil married, it should be to an educated man, one who would respect her wish to keep learning. There was no one like that in the young woman's village, so Sudha searched Bihar for such a person. At last she found a suitable candidate—a young man who wanted to go to law school and would be happy for his wife to keep studying. Her student met him and, happily, she liked him, and they agreed to be married. Afterward she worked as a teacher, and they made their home in her community. She hoped that by staying she might influence others to get educated, like her.

In 2012 Sudha opened another Prerna School in Gaya, funded by the Bihar government and private donors. Soon there were 250 girls at the two schools. She often joked that maybe she was "greedy." She saw so many girls, and she always wanted to help more of them unlock their hidden potential, and discover their talents and worth.

Sudha could see a huge difference between the girls at the two schools—and it showed just how far her first students had come. Whenever she asked the girls at the first school what they wanted to be when they grew up, they would tell her, doctor, teacher, engineer. One girl wanted to be a police officer like her grandfather, the only educated man in her village. But the girls at the new school stared blankly, as if they still couldn't imagine any future other than unskilled labor and domestic chores. The girls at the first school, who had once fixed their eyes on the ground, now met people with confident smiles and greetings, looking them straight in the eye. The new girls had a long way to go to match that level of confidence, but Sudha knew she could get them there.

Agents of Change

Challenges still lie ahead for Prerna's girls. Even educated, once the girls leave the school, their community will still see them first of all as Mushahar—the "rat eaters," the lowest of the low. Sudha knows this but hopes they will have developed the confidence and self-respect to withstand it. "So it's a constant struggle they have to go through," she explains, "to find their own recognition and take their place in the society."

Sudha has a vision for the future, in which each girl will be like a stone thrown in water, sending ripples outward. The girls, changed by education, will in turn change their communities, and society as a whole.

Abandoned buildings are a common sight in Chicago's dangerous West Englewood neighborhood.

GANGS

Caught in the Crossfire

Chicago, Illinois, 2009

In Deonte Tanner's neighborhood, walking to school was a dangerous act. Each morning when the Chicago teenager left his house to go to Harper High School, he passed vacant lots and sidewalks strewn with empty bottles and garbage. Police sirens wailed so frequently that he barely noticed them anymore. But the rundown state of his neighborhood wasn't the problem. Like all the other students starting at Harper High,

Deonte quickly learned not to walk to school alone. Walking in a group was better, and walking in a group down the middle of the road was best.

"We feel safer like this," was how one Harper girl put it. "We never like to walk past trees and stuff, there's too much stuff going on."

She meant that a student walking alone was a target for gunfire. William R. Harper High School was in West Englewood, one of the most dangerous neighborhoods in Chicago's rough South Side. Shootings were commonplace. Gang violence had escalated to the point that every teen who stepped outside was tense and vigilant, waiting for the sound of gunshots. That's when they dropped to the ground.

The school's district was small, but within those city blocks more than 15 gangs claimed a territory. Many teens in Englewood claimed that belonging to a gang was the only way

Police tape marks the site of gun violence in West Englewood.

to survive, that they had no choice. Nearly a third of the families lived below the poverty line, and they couldn't afford to leave. A lot of the kids felt powerless to change their lives for the better, and many would drop out of school before graduating. But Deonte had always seen things differently. All the things that made others hopeless motivated him to want more, for himself and for the people he cared about.

Finding Another Way

When Deonte Tanner started high school at Harper, he made a decision. He would never, ever join a gang. Deonte had another plan in mind. He vowed he would earn the marks he needed to get into college and change his life.

Deonte Tanner, a Harper High student determined to reject gangs and get the college education that will change his life.

Deonte was a smart guy, a good student, but to many it seemed he was taking on an impossible challenge. Many young people in Englewood said there was no avoiding gangs: you were either one of them or one of their victims. As 17-year-old David Ellis said, "The streets are no joke. Some students have been killed trying to walk home from school and some have been shot. I pray that I can finish high school without being a victim of violence." Some felt that gangs at least promised protection—safety in numbers—even if it didn't always work out that way.

But Deonte talked openly about being anti-gang. Soon it was what he was best known for at school, as well as in his neighborhood. Other kids started coming to him for advice. And there was one thing they all wanted to know: How did he expect to do it?

Deonte explained that what he had to do was narrow his focus to the only things that mattered: what it would take to succeed. In his mind, he pictured a triangle imposed over the rough streets of his neighborhood, three lines on which he would concentrate all his attention. "My perfect triangle," he explained, pointing down his street, "is from my house to my school and to my church that's right over there. It's my perfect trinity."

A dedicated Christian, Deonte held Bible study in his living room. He also spent time tutoring eighth-graders. That kept him focused on his goal of becoming a teacher. And there was one more crucial component to his plan: he knew he had to avoid venturing out into the neighborhood after school. Even so, he knew he would be far from safe.

A School under Siege

In Deonte's grade 11 school year, 2011–12, 29 Harper students were shot, and 8 of those young people were killed. At the same time, the number of shootings in the city of Chicago rose alarmingly, with most of the violence happening in the poorest neighborhoods, like Englewood.

Almost all of the violence was caused by gangs. Harper High had become a school under siege, caught in the crossfire of the gang wars raging around it. Many Harper students had witnessed a shooting. They were often traumatized by frightening memories and lived in a tense atmosphere of fear for themselves, their families, and their friends. The shootings rarely happened at school but in the streets surrounding it. The high school itself was a well-tended yellow-brick building, its clean corridors filled with students rushing to class in their uniform red shirts.

The principal, teachers, and social workers there were generally energetic and positive, and they cared very much about their students. Principal Leonetta Sanders in particular was deeply

Shootings, mostly caused by gangs, are alarmingly frequent in the streets around Harper High School.

GANGS AND GUN VIOLENCE

"Our playgrounds have become battlegrounds. Our streets have become cemeteries. Our schools have become places to mourn the ones we've lost." These were the words of President Barack Obama, speaking about the rise in gun violence in cities such as Chicago.

By the end of 2012, Chicago residents were seriously alarmed by the surge in fatal shootings. That year there were 506 homicides in the city, an increase of 16 percent from the previous year. Chicago's police chief placed the blame on gangs operating in certain pockets of the city and on the high number of illegal guns being sold on the street. Police scrambled to respond by increasing the number of officers on patrol in at-risk neighborhoods. They also began a campaign of going door to-door to involve neighbors and intervene with youths known to be linked to gang activity, sometimes getting them and their families in touch with social services.

distressed by the violence her students faced. "We are literally picking up students in the morning in our own cars and bringing them to school because they cannot walk through certain areas," Sanders told a reporter in 2012. "Yesterday morning, for example, I had a student walking down Wood from 63rd to 65th, and he was shot at. He was shot at—*yesterday morning.*"

No More "Neutrons"

Things had changed in recent years in Englewood, especially in the way the local gangs operated. Englewood used to be dominated by a single gang, the Gangster Disciples. But locals said that police arrested so many of its ringleaders that it all but disappeared. In its place, 15 or more gangs sprang up. They often had no leader and attempted to control no more than

Gang violence in Chicago's South Side claims another victim.

a few streets, but many of their members had guns, bought illegally on the street. Shots were fired over disagreements or in retaliation for an earlier shooting. Bystanders were often hurt. Stray bullets even passed through windows and hit people inside their homes.

"It's a war zone around there," one student said, describing the streets surrounding his home. "I can't lie. It's just a war zone . . . Our opposition is right down the street. Literally, it's on the next block."

> "It's a war zone around there. I can't lie. It's just a war zone."
>
> – a Harper High student

According to many Englewood teens, if you lived on a certain street, everyone assumed you belonged to that street's gang. There was no initiation or decision to join. Boys described how, when they reached a certain height and age, rival gangs just started treating them like one of the enemy. Harper's associate principal Chad Adams guessed that few of the high school's students were actually involved in gang-organized crimes such as theft or drug dealing —they were dragged into gang membership simply because of *where they lived*. Students also described how girls often had more choice, and might avoid gangs altogether, but staying out of a gang was much harder—almost impossible—for boys.

There was a time when kids who got high grades or were good at sports were considered neutral in the war. They were called "neutrons," and the gangs pretty much left them alone. But all that had changed, according to a police officer assigned to Harper High. Now there were no more "neutrons."

Still, not everyone agreed that joining a gang was inevitable. Some Chicago teachers said that young men could avoid getting drawn in, but they would have to make tough choices. One of the toughest was to avoid socializing in the neighborhood—not an easy decision for teenagers. Another recommendation was that schools could and should have rules that would keep gang culture from coming through the doors. Otherwise, an unhealthy attitude that "this is just the way things are" could set in and leave students feeling powerless and victimized.

A Terrible Cost

Gang violence and fear took a toll on students' futures. Harper students scored far below average in state standardized tests. In 2014 almost a third of Harper seniors did not graduate. Many just dropped out and became completely absorbed into gang life.

> "Do you know what me and my friends talked about . . . the last day of school? Which one of us won't make it back in August."
>
> – Deonte Tanner

At the end of grade 11, in June 2012, Deonte was talking with Principal Sanders. "Do you know what me and my friends talked about at the end of the school day, the last day of school?" he asked. "Which one of us won't make it back in August."

Sanders asked herself, "What kind of conversation is that for children to have?"

At his Chicago exhibit, artist James Pate invited people to add a tag to a chain-link fence, naming someone they had lost to gun violence. Soon thousands of tags were pinned to the memorial.

That same month, one Saturday evening, a 16-year-old Harper girl named Shakaki Asphy was talking to friends on a porch. Suddenly a youth in a hoodie ran alongside the house and opened fire. Shakaki died of gunshot wounds. She had no connection to any gang; like so many others, she was just in the line of fire. Her family and friends were devastated, overwhelmed with grief, but some were angry as well. Many Harper students and staff went to Shakaki's funeral, where the sound of her mother's anguished weeping drew tears from the hundreds of people packed into the small church. For Principal Sanders, it was the eighth funeral of a Harper student she had attended.

Approaching the Finish Line

The summer of 2012 passed safely for Deonte. Back at Harper in the fall, he and the other returning students passed the memorial Shakaki's friends had made for her in a glass cabinet, with her basketball jersey from the team she loved and a ball signed by her teammates. Some, including a friend who had been at her side when she was shot, couldn't bring themselves to look at it.

It was Deonte's senior year, the one that would decide his future, and he remained resolute. And he was not the only one at Harper. Brittney Knight, a fellow senior, was also determined to defy pressure from gangs and earn the grades she needed for a new life. Like Deonte, she saw herself becoming a teacher some day.

Harper High student Brittney Knight dreamed of earning a scholarship and becoming a teacher.

Deonte was keenly aware that good grades wouldn't solve everything. He came from a large family, and his mom, a single parent, struggled to make ends meet. There was no way his family would ever be able to cover the costs of his university education. Brittney was in a similar situation. She was working hard, aiming for the grades she'd need to get into college. If they succeeded, they would have a new and very serious problem to solve: how to find the money to pay for it.

Getting a scholarship was their only chance. Deonte and Brittney both decided to apply for the Gates Millennium Scholarship, which each year helps 1,000 minority students pay for their post-secondary education at the school of their choice. Offered by the Bill & Melinda Gates Foundation, the scholarships go to students with outstanding grades and leadership potential. It was a prestigious prize, and each year as many as 50,000 motivated students applied.

Was it more than Deonte could hope for? All he could do was concentrate on his grades, put in a strong application, and then wait till the finalists were announced in the spring. And if that didn't work . . . well, he'd just have to find another way. Giving up was not an option for Deonte.

"Not a product of my environment"

Through the fall of his senior year, the isolation Deonte had imposed on himself became hard to bear. A lot of Englewood teens avoided being on the streets outside their house after school and didn't feel safe even on their front porch. But Deonte believed strongly that staying off the street completely was key to avoiding gangs and accomplishing his goal of a university education and a better life. By this time, Deonte almost never went out in his neighborhood at all.

"That can be bad as well," he acknowledged. "Because that's when depression is easy to set in. That took a hold of me, because I've been in the house for about three years. I've been staying in the house a lot." And, he admitted, "At times I feel lonely. At times, I would want to have some friends. Because I'm not really friends with anybody."

But Deonte's commitment to staying away from gang life was total. If that meant barricading himself at home, he would do it.

Throughout Chicago, violence continued to overshadow neighborhoods like Englewood. In January 2013, another teenage girl, Hadiya Pendleton, was killed when two gang members opened fire on a group of her friends, mistaking them for members of a rival gang.

Time after time, when others saw reasons to give up, Deonte saw motivation to work harder, to escape the cycle of violence and fear and failure. "I'm definitely not a product of my environment," he once explained. "Everybody looks at Englewood as if it's disgusting—a savage neighborhood—and for the most part it's true." But not everybody in Englewood was like that, he insisted, "with no life and no hope. And I'm showing people that there's a difference."

And so was Brittney. Her hard work was paying off. She was sitting in the school lunchroom after report cards had been handed out in mid-April when a voice boomed above her, making every head turn.

"Straight A student right here! Straight A's! All A's! Brittney Knight!"

An anonymous plea to end gang violence

It was a friendly Harper staff member, grinning and pointing to Brittney.

Brittney had mixed feelings about the attention. "Oh my gosh, he's embarrassing me, putting me on blast!" she said. "But I like it though."

The same month, Deonte got a letter in the mail. It was from the Gates Foundation. All his years of struggle had been leading up to this moment.

"I opened the folder," he said. "It's like, 'Congratulations.' That's all I had to see, and I just fell out—just 'Congratulations.'"

He was a Gates Millennium Scholar, and now he could afford to go to any college in the country. He could even complete a graduate degree with full financial support. At first it seemed

"You don't have to be an athlete or a drug dealer to make it out of this neighborhood. As long as you've got the will and the hope and the belief in yourself, then you can do it."

– Deonte Tanner

too good to be true. The news came "right on time" for him, he said.

"My mom is a single parent and there [are] seven of us at home. I don't have a job to help out but thank God for this blessing," he said. "After college I want to use my education to help people that are struggling. I grew up in Englewood watching people struggle and I want to change that."

Brittney got her letter, too. She was working her shift at McDonald's when she received the good news. Like Deonte, she was overjoyed: the scholarship overcame her final obstacle. "It lifted a big burden off our shoulders, because we were just talking about how much in loans we were going to take out, and what we were going to pay out of pocket, and then this came. It was a blessing."

Brittney and Deonte were the first Harper students ever to win the scholarship.

After that, everything changed for Deonte. Suddenly he had more possibilities open to him than ever before. By the end of the month, he had narrowed his choices down to Marquette University in Wisconsin or the University of Denver. He still wanted to be an elementary school teacher. His days tutoring grade 8 students had made a big impression on him, and he liked helping kids. And he started dreaming about how he could change not only his own life but the lives of other people in Englewood.

"If I'm able to run a health center or a hope center, then that's more kids' lives that I can possibly impact and possibly change," he told reporters who interviewed him about the scholarship.

"Let them know that we hear them, we see them"

During Deonte's last year of high school, the violence engulfing Harper High and Englewood had been drawing wider attention. The public radio show *This American Life* sent reporters to the school over the course of five months to document the lives of students and staff caught in the gang war zone. News of Harper's desperate situation spread, and the stories prompted First Lady Michelle Obama to visit the school racked by violence in her hometown of Chicago.

In April 2013 Mrs. Obama met with 22 Harper students in the second-floor library. Deonte was one of them. She talked to them about life in Englewood and asked how many of them had been personally affected by gun violence. All of them had. For two hours, she encouraged them to talk about it.

"She's no stranger to the streets," one 18-year-old girl said of Obama. "She told us how she grew up on the South Side, and while it was not as violent as it is now, it was still dangerous for her." Obama stressed how much the Harper students were like her at that age. As she had said before, "Hadiya Pendleton was me, and I was her." The students found her "down to earth" and felt encouraged and motivated by the talk.

First Lady Michelle Obama greets students from Harper High.

Afterward Obama described how she had listened to teens "share their stories of how every day they wake up and they wonder whether they're going to make it out of school alive. I mean, every single one worried about their own death, or the death of someone, every single day."

"One kid told me he felt like he lived in a cage because he feels like his community is unseen, unheard, and nobody cares about it," Obama later said to reporters. "What's our obligation to these kids? We do have one."

The Harper kids weren't alone, she pointed out. Their experience was part of a wider problem in the poor neighborhoods of many American cities.

"We have millions of kids living in these kind of circumstances who are doing everything right," Obama said, "and we, as a nation, have to embrace these kids and let them know that we hear them, we see them."

The visit meant a great deal to Deonte. "She motivated me a lot with what she said," he explained. "She talked about how the best things in life are hard to come by, like an education, and that if we stay strong, we could conquer anything that comes our way."

"A once-in-a-lifetime experience"

Mrs. Obama was so impressed by the students at Harper High that, before leaving, she invited them to visit the White House and meet President Obama. Some of the kids were skeptical. They figured she was just being polite. But when Principal Sanders handed out the permission forms for parents to sign, Deonte and the others knew it was actually going to happen. A local law firm paid for the trip, and in June Deonte Tanner was one of 24 students who traveled to Washington, D.C. They had lunch with the president and first lady, talked about their lives and challenges, and spent the day at the White House.

Most of the students were surprised by how relaxed the meeting was. David Ellis was one of them. "The president . . . gave us high fives, asked us about the type of music we listen to and who are some of our heroes in life," he said. "I could hang out with him any day." Most important, the teens felt motivated by the meeting. Someone out there cared about the challenges they faced; someone believed they could overcome them.

"It still does not seem real," Deonte said afterward. "It was a once-in-a-lifetime experience for me and one I will always remember."

While in Washington, Deonte and the others also visited Howard University, a historically black university with many prestigious graduates. Deonte was so impressed that he briefly considered going to college there instead. The whole experience seemed to open his eyes to the world of possibilities before him. Nothing seemed impossible anymore.

"I was all set to go to Marquette University to study political science, but now I'm thinking Howard," he said enthusiastically. "I plan to run for elected office when I finish graduate school. Maybe even the presidency. Then I could invite Harper students back to the White House."

Deonte had one more honor in store for him that June: he was chosen to be class valedictorian. And in the end he decided to stick to his original plan—that fall, he began his college life at Marquette University in Wisconsin.

"If Deonte can do it, so can I"

Perhaps one of the most important successes that Deonte and Brittney achieved was how they inspired younger students at Harper High and other Chicago schools.

One of those students was Deonte's own cousin, Anthony Boyd. He was in grade 8 and headed for Harper when Deonte got his scholarship. "If [Deonte] can do it, so can I," he said. "And that's not because he is my cousin. It is because I know anything is possible with hard work."

Another Harper student, 16-year-old Britany Robinson, was also inspired to try for the Gates scholarship and pursue her dream of becoming a pediatrician. Medical school had always seemed out of her reach, but not anymore. "No one living around here really expects us to go to college, especially coming

Harper High students talk with President Obama during their visit to the White House.

out of Harper. But they're wrong to think that, and Deonte and Brittney are proof of it."

There are other promising signs of change in Englewood. The city has invested more in summer jobs, mentoring, and recreation programs for young people who might otherwise get caught up in gang life. The goals of the programs are to keep at-risk boys out of gangs and help them focus on getting an education and building lives for themselves. The city's mayor has encouraged business leaders to invest in these life-saving programs.

One new program has had exceptional success. The B.A.M. (Becoming a Man) program mentors and guides boys in danger of dropping out of school and getting involved in violent crime. Group exercises and sports are used to teach important life skills, such as how to resolve conflict without violence and how to set aspirations and goals. B.A.M. based its approach on research that showed much of the city's fatal gun violence resulted from impulsive behavior: "young people with access to guns 'massively' over-reacting." The B.A.M. leaders hope to change that pattern. The results have been encouraging: the statistics show that B.A.M. members are already less likely to engage in crime and more likely to graduate from high school.

Sixteen-year-old R.J. Howard gave B.A.M. credit for allowing him to escape the pressure of gangs. "It is a life-saver, for sure,"

Members of the successful B.A.M. (Becoming a Man) program talk with the president about helping Chicago youth avoid gangs and build better lives for themselves.

he said. "I cannot imagine what type of man I would be if I were not involved with B.A.M." He says it's helping him complete his goal of graduating and going to college.

Students like Deonte and Brittney have already shown the way. Principal Sanders believed Harper High's first two Gates Millennium Scholarship winners would prove to everyone else that there was much more to Harper than a cycle of violence and failure.

When asked how she felt about Deonte and Brittney's awards, at first Sanders seemed too overwhelmed for words, saying, "Just so proud, so proud, so proud."

Then she added, "'Cause it really shows how, even in the midst of so many issues and challenges, students can still prevail and move on and do great things."

Children as young as eight have been abducted by rebel armies in Africa.

WAR

Forced into Battle

UGANDA, 1985

Sixteen-year-old Okello Kelo Sam should have been sitting in a classroom at the start of a new school year. Instead he was marching north, exhausted and dazed from hunger, with a rebel army. He was not there by choice. Okello was one of thousands of Ugandan children kidnapped by the rebels and forced to fight in their army or carry their loads.

The country had experienced several episodes of violent political upheaval since dictator Idi Amin was overthrown in 1979. Rival factions fought for power, often waging vicious

Young boys captured by rebel armies undergo brutal training and brainwashing, and are forced to use weapons.

guerrilla warfare to seize control, with terrible consequences for the people of Uganda.

Okello and his friends had been on their way to school when they were captured. They were being cautious, as always—they had all heard about the rebel Uganda National Liberation Army raiding villages and abducting children. Classes were over for the year, but the boys were eager to see their test results and find out if they had passed into the next grade. They never got there. Now they were being taken north to the rebel army's camp in Sudan. Soon they would be split up, dragged to different war fronts.

Okello had heard rumors that some children had been able to get away. All he could do now was try to survive and hope for a chance to escape.

UGANDA'S CHILD SOLDIERS

An army using children as soldiers is a horrifying idea, and yet it has been a reality for years in some war-torn areas, especially in African countries such as Uganda, Sudan, Central African Republic, Chad, and Democratic Republic of Congo. Almost all of these children, some as young as eight, have been kidnapped and forced to either fight or work as porters, cooks, and spies. Most child soldiers are abducted by rebel armies, but some government armies have used children as well.

Why do armies use children as soldiers? According to the charitable organization War Child, rebel armies have found children useful for many reasons, including that they eat less than adults, they can be manipulated with brainwashing, and they do not yet have an adult's fully formed sense of danger.

In 2012 six of the eight countries known to recruit children in their armies committed to stopping the practice. In 2013 the United Nations set a goal of a world without child soldiers by 2016.

After enduring the torture and brainwashing of his first two weeks of training, Okello's ordeal dragged on for another eighteen months—or maybe it was two years. He lost track of time. In later years, Okello never wanted to discuss what happened during those months. But if his experience was typical of other child soldiers, he was likely terrorized and beaten into obedience, and forced to use weapons and commit acts of violence.

Then one day his group was ordered into a battle against government forces. The fight was chaotic, and in the midst of the mayhem, Okello saw his chance. He ran from the scene of the fighting, his heart pounding ferociously, scarcely believing that this might be his escape at last.

Free, he made his way slowly homeward, always hiding and watching carefully to evade recapture. He wanted desperately to find his family and let them know he was alive, and he prayed that they were unharmed. But as he got closer, he discovered that his once beautiful and peaceful homeland in Northern Uganda had become a chaotic war zone. People told him not to bother returning to his village; it was deserted. He should look for his family in the city of Gulu, they said, where many people had fled to take shelter from the conflict.

Okello jumped onto the back of a truck headed to Gulu, but when he arrived, his family was nowhere to be found. What could he do now? The only thing left was to go back to his village, deserted or not, to look for them. He and a few companions he'd met hitched a ride on a convoy of trucks. Together they crowded into the back of one of the trucks, which was already loaded with canisters of paraffin for lamps, and headed for his village—and the very heart of the war zone.

Former child soldiers get some much-needed sleep at a refugee camp, after being kept on the move in the wilderness by roving armies.

The countryside through which they traveled was now the territory of another roaming army: the Holy Spirit Movement, a group of violent rebels bent on overthrowing the government. Its members ambushed the truck, opening fire. Pierced by bullets, the canisters spurted hot paraffin. Okello and the other travelers were now in terrible pain, burned by the fuel. The convoy sped on and escaped the ambush. But there would be no stopping near his village now—Okello had to stay on the truck as it drove on to Kampala, the capital.

He remembered his family talking with pride about an uncle in Kampala, a man who made a good living. Okello had never met the man. He knew only his name, Odongo, and the company he worked for. Hopping off in Kampala, he began his search. Even if he could find him, Okello had no idea if this relative he'd never met would help him, but he had nowhere else to turn.

Tenacious in his search, Okello did at last locate Uncle Odongo. It seemed the stories of his success had been a little exaggerated. He was a driving-school instructor who lived with his family in a two-room house in one of the city's slums. But Odongo let Okello move in and gave him a mat on the floor for his bed. That was enough for Okello to start his life over.

Reclaiming a Life

Okello worked however he could to raise money: carrying water, washing clothes, cleaning cars. Little by little, he saved for one purpose: to go back to school and finish the education that had been stolen from him. Word got to him that members of his family had been able to return to their village, but his uncle found a place for him in a Kampala school, and he got back on track there.

Okello finished high school and went on to university, pursuing his two loves: theater and learning. While still in school, he had seen a theater performance by Ndere Troupe, a popular group that celebrated traditional Ugandan dance and music, and Okello was captivated. He even convinced the director to let him join the company.

Okello's life in those days was happy. In Kampala, he was far away from the fighting. He got married, and he began to have success as a performer and actor. But at the same time, the turmoil in Uganda continued. The Holy Spirit Movement, whose men had attacked the truck on the road home, had been defeated and its leader sent into exile. But the rebel group was about to reemerge, under a new leader, as the Lord's Resistance Army.

THE LORD'S RESISTANCE ARMY

The Lord's Resistance Army (LRA) started in Northern Uganda in the 1980s as a rebel movement fighting to overthrow the government. During the next 20 years, it became a violent and brutal force that attacked innocent civilians. Arrest warrants for its leaders were issued by the International Criminal Court in 2005. Driven out of Uganda by the government in the mid-2000s, the LRA continued to operate as a terrorist group in bordering countries.

The United Nations estimated that from 1987 to 2012, the LRA kidnapped up to 100,000 children and displaced more than 2.5 million civilians.

Many Ugandan villages were destroyed by the Lord's Resistance Army.

In 1996 Okello heard devastating news. His teenage brother Godfrey, who had been going to high school in Gulu, had been kidnapped by the LRA. They had raided his boarding school, abducting 50 children. For a while, Okello took hope from occasional rumors that his brother was still alive.

Then one day Okello opened a newspaper to read about a brutal attack by the LRA on his own village that had left many of his relatives and friends dead. Overcome, he got into his car with one intention: to go home. A friend who was with him worried about Okello's desperate state of mind, and he insisted on joining him. As Okello sped northward, his friend begged him to turn back, trying to convince him that it was crazy to head back into the middle of the war. Northern Uganda was a countryside scarred by the fighting, a landscape of burned schools, destroyed homes and villages, and ruined fields.

Okello later remembered that this incident changed his life. "When I got the news, I just broke down," he said. "I had to do something. So I get into my car, driving toward the north, just doing it out of anger, out of frustration; so many of the people you know have died, and you don't know what else to do. So we kept on driving, driving, driving and I stopped.

"And an idea came to my mind."

Hope North

Okello saw with a flash of clarity that it was the children of Uganda who could make peace a reality. But they couldn't do it as long as the war kept them ignorant and enslaved. "To build the conditions for peace," he realized, "we must educate and empower youth."

> "To build the conditions for peace, we must educate and empower youth."
>
> — Okello Kelo Sam

Okello bought land in a safe district, away from the fighting, in northwestern Uganda. He had a new dream now. He would build a haven for the children who'd been hurt by war, as he had been. It would be a place where orphans, escaped child soldiers, and refugees could go back to school.

For some child soldiers who had escaped, there was no going home. They were no longer welcome in their villages and old schools. People believed they had become dangerous and could be incited by the rebel leaders to violence once more.

Former child soldiers make a new start by reclaiming the education stolen from them.

Okello hoped he could give these children both a refuge and the education they needed to reclaim their lives. He would build a high school, and they would get job training. War had robbed thousands of children of their education; he wanted to give it back to them.

The plot of land became a hive of construction as a village rose up: cottages, classrooms, dormitories, a vocational school. A bakery and plots of farmland would help to make the project self-sustaining. Okello called his campus Hope North.

"Children who experience terrible things can also achieve great things in life—if they are given an education."

– former Ugandan girl soldier

Children uprooted by war overcome their trauma and find a sense of belonging through dance.

Okello believed strongly in the power of the arts to heal the pain many children still suffered from their experiences. He was now himself a well-known performer of traditional African music and dance, and he encouraged children to join in dance, music, and drama in addition to their academic studies, as a way of moving beyond war and suffering.

Whenever Okello explained his project, his enthusiasm and passion became obvious. His tall, thin frame seemed to crackle with energy. "I try to provide them with instruments so they can make music, and especially drums," he said. "The drums have so much power to release energy." Ugandan music and dance, he believed, also helped displaced children "to know that now they are back to their roots, their culture." For children torn

Okello Kelo Sam with one of Hope North's supporters,
American actor Susan Sarandon

from home, this sense of belonging was precious. He found that
the children who joined in did better in school. And they had
fewer nightmares.

In the following years, Hope North grew by leaps and
bounds. Word spread of the project, and donations helped it
flourish. Today Okello describes how the number of children
and families coming to the campus "keeps growing, day and
night." Many arrive with nothing but a battered suitcase. Since
its start, over 3,000 children and youths have found a refuge
there. And Hope North's secondary school is now fully ac-
credited, with 28 Ugandan teachers and 250 students working
toward degrees and careers.

Former child soldiers in Somalia are handed over to UNICEF, which will help them begin new lives.

Healing the Wounds of War

Since the LRA was driven from the country, positive changes have come to Northern Uganda. More than 95 percent of the people displaced by the rebel army have left refugee camps and returned homeward to rebuild their lives. Since 2000, more than 12,000 former LRA soldiers and kidnapped youths are known to have left the army and, granted amnesty by Uganda, returned to a life in society. In addition, countless others have escaped and returned to their villages without reporting to officials.

Besides Hope North, other projects have been started throughout Uganda aimed at helping the children whose lives and education were derailed by war. Anywar Ricky Richard, a former child soldier who was kidnapped by the LRA at age 14, also escaped his captors and eventually finished school. After graduating from university, he founded Friends of Orphans, an organization run by former child soldiers that seeks to help other children scarred by war—whether they are orphans, refugees, or former soldiers themselves.

Ricky had felt a strong desire to help other children like him while he was still a captive of the LRA, on the move in the wilderness. "The idea came to me when I was in the bush," he recalled. "I kept thinking that I wanted to help, but I didn't know there was such a thing as . . . a group that would help. I was a child, so I just thought, 'If I escape, I will take care of one person, keep him from dying.'"

Once their ordeals are over, many of the children Ricky has met are in a state of shock, traumatized and urgently needing medical and psychological care. Ricky is successful in helping them largely because his own experiences have given him a full understanding of their suffering and difficulty readjusting. Being former child soldiers themselves, members of Friends of Orphans have the insight to help.

The mission of Ricky's group is to welcome the children back into normal life and restore their confidence through education, health, and peace-building skills. Ricky gives credit to his own education for "transforming me from a child soldier to someone of value in the community." Because many former child soldiers grew up in the bush and were kept illiterate, Friends of Orphans focuses on teaching them employable skills, such as tailoring, bricklaying, mechanics, and carpentry. They also learn management skills, so they can start their own businesses. Like Okello, Ricky emphasizes reconciliation among Ugandans as a means of undoing the damage of war.

As for Okello, he feels his goals are simple—and attainable: "All I want is to be able to use performance arts to advocate for peace and reconciliation, and to help as many African children as possible receive an education. That is enough for me."

"All I want is to be able to use performance arts to advocate for peace and reconciliation, and to help as many African children as possible receive an education. That is enough for me."

— Okello Kelo Sam

4

PROTEST
MOVEMENTS

"You may have heard the story of ...
Rosa Parks ... we are the children who
have been sitting at the back of the
school bus our whole lives, and we
don't want to stay there anymore."

– Chelsea Edwards

Thirteen-year-old activist Shannen Koostachin talks to a crowd of supporters on Parliament Hill.

EQUAL SCHOOLS

Shannen Koostachin: The Right to a "Real School"

Ottawa, Ontario, June 2008

On the steps outside the Parliament Buildings in Canada's capital, a 13-year-old Cree girl walked up to a microphone. Before her, thousands of people were gathered for a rally, waiting expectantly. She was a long way from her home in Attawapiskat, a remote First Nation reserve in Northern Ontario on the shores of James Bay.

Shannen Koostachin had traveled all the way to Ottawa for one reason. Along with a handful of classmates, parents, and elders from her reserve, she was here to challenge the Minister of Indian Affairs with a question: Why don't the children of Attawapiskat have a school like the ones other Canadian children have? Why has the government broken its promises?

Earlier, in their meeting with Indian Affairs minister Chuck Strahl, Shannen had demonstrated the outspoken manner that was already making her a leader. To break the ice with the delegates, Strahl had asked how they liked his office. Shannen glanced around the room. The contrast to the cold, mouse-infested portable she went to class in could not have been greater.

"I wish my brothers and sisters had a classroom as nice as this," she blurted out.

Now, as Shannen and her companions stood in the June sunshine, they did not have good news for the crowd of supporters on the lawn of Parliament Hill. The Indian Affairs minister had told them there would be no new school for their reserve. Glancing at the band elders next to her, Shannen saw some had tears in their eyes. For her part, she felt confused and disappointed, but she refused to let it show.

When it was her turn to speak, there was no sign of discouragement in her face, just stubborn determination. Wearing her "National Day of Action" T-shirt, her long, dark hair pulled back in pigtails, Shannen adjusted the microphone and addressed the sea of expectant faces.

"When I shook Chuck Strahl's hand, I looked him in the eye, and I could tell he was nervous," she said. "I told him, 'We're not going away. We're not giving up.'"

The crowd broke into applause and cheers. Those who knew Shannen well knew she meant every word.

Left Out in the Cold

At the age of 13, Shannen Koostachin realized she had never seen a "real school."

For 8 years, Shannen, along with 400 other students on her reserve, had been going to class in portables. Now in grade 8, she looked around her at the overcrowded, makeshift buildings, which looked like scattered metal sheds, battered by wind and snow. In winter many of her classmates kept their parkas on during class, as the portables were drafty and cold. Freezing and thawing had caused the bases of the portables to shift, and doors gaped permanently ajar. Icy winds whistled through the many broken windows.

"It's hard to concentrate in class when you're always shivering!" her friends would complain.

To make matters worse, mice took refuge in the buildings, and the students' lunches and snacks were always at risk of being nibbled. Each portable had a single washroom, embarrassingly close to the desks. Shannen was often distracted from what the teacher was saying by the constant sounds of running water and flushing. And there was no library, no music room, no science lab, no cafeteria.

When it was time to move to the next class, students braced themselves for the cold outside—there were no corridors between classrooms! The walk all the way to the community center for gym was the bitterest. They just had to bundle up and brave the weather outside, even if there was a blizzard or freezing rain. In January, the daytime temperature regularly dipped to −30° Celsius (−22° Fahrenheit).

Shannen could barely remember when Attawapiskat First Nation had a proper elementary school. The federal government

Attawapiskat First Nation reserve in Northern Ontario, where Shannen grew up

had built it in 1976, but almost immediately the problems had started. Unknown to anyone, a diesel fuel pipe buried under the school ruptured. Like an invisible enemy, the toxic fumes leached into every classroom. Environmental investigators came to the site and announced that there was a serious health risk, and finally in 2000 the chief and council of Attawapiskat First Nation ordered the school closed for good. In time it was demolished, and the toxic area was fenced in.

Shannen was just starting school then, and everyone expected that the government would give them a brand-new building. Instead, eleven portables were set up between the contaminated ground and an airstrip. They were told it was a temporary solution, but, as an Attawapiskat leader would later say of the community's housing problems, "Temporary has a way of becoming permanent around here."

Like the portables where Shannen went to school, housing in Attawapiskat was often inadequate.

Years passed, and a generation of kids were growing up in the portables, waiting for a school that never materialized. Three different government ministers promised on different occasions that there would be a new school. But still nothing happened.

As Shannen's friend Chelsea Edwards would later wonder, "How could this happen in a country like Canada?"

Shannen could see the effect these conditions were having on her schoolmates. By the time they got to grade 4, a lot of students were already skipping classes. Soon many kids were falling behind. And more than half dropped out altogether before finishing high school, too discouraged to continue. Shannen knew that when people didn't get a high school diploma, they had trouble getting a good job. School life in the portables was hard on the teachers, too. With classes split up among the isolated portables, the teachers felt alone and quickly burned out. Many left after just a year or two.

AN UNFAIR GAP

Canada's federal government is responsible for paying for schools on First Nation reserves. This has long been guaranteed by treaties. Yet there has been an unfair gap in quality between schools for non-native children and those for native children living on reserves. Why? Many reserves are in isolated northern locations, and the costs of building and operating a school there are high. At the same time, 40 percent of First Nations students go to a school off their reserve, so a considerable chunk of government funding goes to pay for costs there. In 2009 the First Nations Education Council reported that actual spending on the 70,000 students who go to school on their reserves was well below the national average. Clearly the government's approach to funding First Nations schools was falling far short of what was needed.

As a result, reserve schools are often overcrowded, run down, and unsafe. Health hazards abound: mold, high carbon dioxide levels, and sewage fumes. Most also lack basic resources other schools take for granted—libraries, computers, gyms, labs. According to the federal government, as of 2010, 48 new schools were needed on First Nation reserves across the country, and 29 existing schools required major renovations.

> "I had to leave half of myself back at home, my identity, my language, my family, my friends."
>
> — Chelsea Edwards, Attawapiskat student who attended high school in Timmins, Ontario

Attawapiskat had a high school, but promising students would often leave the reserve to attend one that was better funded. They might board with a family hundreds of kilometers south in an Ontario city such as Timmins. Shannen understood why they went, but she also knew that going away to a non-native high school meant giving up a lot: an education based in Cree culture, the support of family and friends, home. Many didn't last long, away from the close-knit community they had always known. But for anyone who wanted a good education, it was the only way. Ambitious students faced a brutal choice: stay and get a poor education, or leave behind everything that matters.

A good student herself, Shannen knew that if she wanted to follow her dream of becoming a lawyer, she would have to do the same. Starting next year, she would have to live with the homesickness and the long weeks away from her family. It seemed wrong. Why couldn't she go to a school near home and still follow her dream?

The Fight for a Real School Begins

In 2007 plans were approved and it looked like it was really going to happen—a new school for Attawapiskat! But late that year there was a change at Indian Affairs, and the new minister, Chuck Strahl, scrapped the school project. Apparently it was not in the government's five-year capital plan because of "other priorities."

For Shannen, the bad news was a call to action. Her older sister Serena had been helping to campaign for a better school ever since grade 7. Now Shannen joined her sister's efforts, and her charisma and energy soon made her a leader. She had an inspiring belief that nothing was impossible. In a place where many had lost hope, her optimism was contagious.

What Shannen wanted for the kids in her community was simple: "safe and comfy schools" based in First Nations culture.

The cancellation of the new school incited Shannen to march in her first protest. Children and teens held a demonstration outside the portables in the snow. The temperature plunged to −40º Celsius (−40º Fahrenheit) that day, and they were 400 kilometers (248 miles) from any media, but local people took pictures.

Shannen, her sister, and friends uploaded videos on YouTube to show the world outside of Attawapiskat what life was like for the children on the reserve. If everyone knew what was really going on, they would never let it continue—Shannen was sure of that. She addressed a poignant video to Chuck Strahl. In it, Shannen pieced together images, words, and music to plead for a new school. She showed pictures of the tiny classrooms and the gaping doors. Footage of their protest showed the children standing

Shannen's sister and fellow education activist Serena Koostachin

Students organize and protest on Parliament Hill in Ottawa
for equal education for First Nations.

Shannen (right) and other Attawapiskat teens spread awareness of their
new-school campaign with speeches and online videos.

in the snow and holding a sign that read, "We've never seen a real school, and if the government has its way, we never will."

The video caught the attention of students at non-native Ontario schools, who started writing letters of protest to the government on behalf of Attawapiskat. A movement called Students Helping Students grew. Adults joined their cause, too, including Cindy Blackstock, an activist from the Gitxsan First Nation. And at least one Member of Parliament (MP) was on their side. Charlie Angus, who represented the people of Timmins–James Bay, badgered Strahl in the House of Commons with questions about the children's plight. The support was encouraging; it meant they weren't alone.

Shannen knew this wasn't just a fight for Attawapiskat. Other reserves, not just in Ontario but all across Canada, had broken-down schools, or no schools at all. In Lake St. Martin, Manitoba, students had been forced to flee a derelict school infested with snakes, and they'd been stuck in portables for 10 years, waiting for a new building. In a way, a new school in Attawapiskat was a symbol for education on all reserves. Shannen wanted to fight for all those students, too.

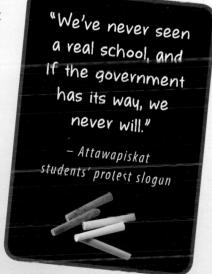

"We've never seen a real school, and if the government has its way, we never will."

– Attawapiskat students' protest slogan

The campaign reached a high point on that day in June 2008 when Shannen and her fellow advocates got their big chance to meet face to face with Strahl in Ottawa. He listened to their plea, but he turned them down. Other priorities had pushed the new school off his department's agenda, he said. He claimed the portables were "not a health and safety risk" for the children. He had to prioritize spending based on health and safety, he insisted, and there were other schools in worse shape.

Shannen was unimpressed by his opinion of the portables. "I don't think he should be saying they're safe till he has walked in our moccasins," she told the crowd outside on Parliament Hill that day.

The minister's refusal was a shattering blow, and the delegation from the reserve was pushed close to despair. But Shannen did not lose her stubborn persistence. She trusted in the momentum of all the people who were on their side. They would get their new school. It was only a matter of time, she believed.

"A chance to grow up to be somebody"

Shannen and other young activists decided to travel to spread the word beyond Attawapiskat. In November 2008 she and her fellow students stood before a gathering of youth leaders and educators in Toronto. When she took the microphone, she spoke simply and got straight to the point.

"Hello. My name is Shannen Koostachin and I am from the Attawapiskat First Nation. I would like to talk to you about what it is like to be a child who grows up never seeing a real school."

By that time Shannen had done a lot of public speaking, but it still made her nervous. And speaking in English made her even more uncomfortable than speaking in Cree. She spoke quickly at first, reading much of her prepared speech, but as she continued her voice grew stronger and more determined. And her honesty shone through.

Shannen discovers her "gift to move people with words":
speaking at a youth forum in Toronto.

"It's hard to feel pride when your classrooms are cold, and the mice run over our lunches. It's hard to feel like you could have a chance to grow up to be somebody important when you don't have proper resources like libraries and science labs. You know that kids in other communities have proper schools. So you begin to feel as if you are a child who doesn't count for anything . . .

"We want our younger brothers and sisters to go to school thinking that school is a time for hopes and dreams of the future. Every kid deserves this."

Those who heard her speak were impressed. Shannen began to discover that she had what her father called "a special gift to move people with words."

"I'm on my own"

When it was time for Shannen to start grade 9, she resolved to leave Attawapiskat to get a better high school education than she could at home. Together with her sister Serena, she moved 600 kilometers (373 miles) south to New Liskeard, Ontario, to attend the local high school. The sisters first stayed with the family of MP Charlie Angus, who continued to support their cause, and then later with another family.

Grade 9 was hard. Shannen had trouble keeping up at first, and that made her all the more painfully aware of how inadequate her schooling had been up till then. She worried, and she missed her family terribly. But she also knew that other kids whose families couldn't afford to send them away from home didn't even have the choice she'd been given. And she felt very lucky to be at a "real school" at last: one with a library and a gym and computers.

While she struggled to catch up in class, she kept campaigning for the new school back home—one for her younger brothers and sisters, cousins, and friends. She didn't want to watch *them* grow up going to school in "washrooms," as she called the portables. Shannen and Serena toured schools in the area, speaking to classes and encouraging students to write letters to the government. As they made their way through each school's hallways, Shannen often lagged behind, peeking into classrooms—real schools

> "School is a time for hopes and dreams of the future. Every kid deserves this."
>
> – Shannen Koostachin

fascinated her, and she wanted to see as much as she could.

"No child should have to walk in my moccasins again."

– Shannen Koostachin

In November 2009 Shannen and Serena joined MP Charlie Angus to speak at a meeting of the Ontario Federation of Labour. The OFL, a group made up of Ontario's unions, represented a lot of ordinary working Canadians, and Angus thought the union leaders might become new allies in the fight for a school. News reporters would be there, too.

By now Shannen had lost her nervousness when speaking to a crowd. She didn't read a prepared speech anymore; instead she took her time and spoke directly about how she felt about the years in the school portables, waiting. She also spoke honestly about what it was like having to live without her family just to get a proper education.

"You know, every day I would have to call home because at times I would get homesick. And when they would have to go, I couldn't hang up, because every time I hang up I get that cold feeling that I'm on my own." More than once, Shannen had to stop mid-sentence, too emotional to go on. At each pause there was complete silence in the room; her audience of tough-minded union leaders was hanging on her every word.

As Angus described it, the sisters "walked out of that room with the commitment of every union in Ontario backing the campaign to build a school—it was amazing. She was just so honest and so raw, and that's how people knew she was real."

The world outside Canada took notice, too. In 2009, when Shannen was just 14, she was nominated for the International

Children's Peace Prize—an annual award that recognizes a child whose courageous actions have advanced children's rights.

When she learned that she'd been nominated, Shannen wrote a letter describing what she was fighting for. She wrote that she would do whatever she could to support non-native students, too, because "we are all the same." And she added that there were "three other things I would like people to know about me: one, I do not like broken promises. Two, I do not like seeing my siblings going to school in washrooms. And three, I would like them to know too that I AM NOT GIVING UP."

"You have the power to change the world, like Shannen did"

Closer to home, Shannen was thrilled when her high school asked her to lead the dance at the annual powwow. She loved taking part in Cree dances, with the traditional garments in her own special colors—light blue, white, and black—twirling around her. But Shannen would never take her place that year among the dancers.

In May 2010 Shannen went on a holiday to Ottawa with a family friend and two schoolmates—a well-earned reward for her success in grade 10. On the journey home, their van was hit by a truck on a remote stretch of road. Both Shannen and the family friend were killed.

Back home, her family and community were shattered. "She was one of our upcoming young leaders," Chief Theresa Hall said when she heard the news. "We are still in a state of shock, we really can't believe it."

After some debate, and with the permission of Shannen's family, it was decided that the powwow would go ahead as planned, but it would be held in her honor. As the drummers pounded and the dancers made their way around the grounds in the grand entry, an empty space was left for Shannen.

Shannen's father, Andrew Koostachin, asked Charlie Angus to speak at Shannen's funeral. Angus decided to let Shannen's own words speak for her instead, reading from the letter she wrote to the Peace Prize committee. Then he added, "We see the footprints where Shannen was walking. We know where she wanted her community to go . . . She told us again and again, 'I am not giving up,' and so we can't give up . . . She was passionate about education. She believed in the youth of this community . . . You have the power to change the world, like Shannen did."

Shannen's Dream: A Call to Action

Many of the young people Shannen had inspired decided there was only one thing to do: pick up where she had left off and carry on the fight for a new school in her name. Serena Koostachin and Shannen's friend Chelsea Edwards joined with Chris Kataquapit and other teens to create a nationwide campaign for equal education for First Nations children. In November 2010, they named their cause Shannen's Dream. They called on schoolchildren to organize letter-writing teams and send their letters to Prime Minister Stephen Harper, to call their Members of Parliament, and to sign online petitions.

At the same time, Charlie Angus introduced a motion in the House of Commons. Although it was officially Motion 571, everyone called it the Shannen's Dream motion. It called on the government to invest as much in the education of each First Nations child as it did for other Canadian children and to work with First Nations leaders on an action plan to make

Young volunteers join the Shannen's Dream movement.

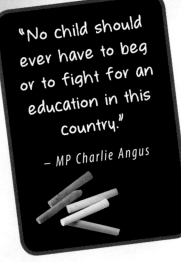

"No child should ever have to beg or to fight for an education in this country."

– MP Charlie Angus

sure students on reserves had well-funded schools based in their culture. If it passed, it would guarantee that First Nations children had the right to high-quality education, relevant to their culture, in schools that were the equal of non-reserve provincial schools.

"No child should ever have to beg or to fight for an education in this country," Angus declared.

The youth team behind Shannen's Dream called for a national day of action, rallying students and teachers from as many schools as possible to march on Parliament in Ottawa, demanding that the government support equal educational rights for First Nations children. On April 27, 2011, the gathering on Parliament Hill was beyond anything the team had expected. Hundreds of students came, pulling wagons full of letters, some stored in small-scale models of a new school for Attawapiskat.

"Someone out there is listening"

Shannen's Dream was gaining support, and pressure for change was building within Canada. But Serena and the others knew there would have to be pressure from outside as well to get the attention of the politicians in Ottawa.

In February 2012 six aboriginal teens from across Canada, including Chelsea Edwards, flew to Geneva to talk to the United Nations Committee on the Rights of the Child. The committee would soon review how well Canada was complying with its obligations under the United Nations Convention on the Rights of the Child, especially the right to education. The six youth ambassadors hoped pressure from the United Nations would convince the government that the time for change was now. In Geneva Chelsea

Shannen's Dream cofounder Chelsea Edwards

and the others each had a chance to tell their stories to the committee members. Chelsea explained just how dire her reserve's schools were, and how she believed this violated her most basic rights. Afterward, she felt proud. "Someone out there is listening to us," she said with satisfaction.

First Nations activist Cindy Blackstock felt confident the time for change had come at last. It was no longer a question of whether or not the government would do the right thing, she declared. "Canada will treat First Nations kids with the justice and equity they deserve. The only question is how embarrassed [does it] want to be when [it does] it."

Everything was building toward one crucial event. On February 27, 2012, Parliament would vote at last on the Shannen's Dream motion. Shannen's parents, her sister Serena, and Chelsea Edwards traveled to Ottawa to be there.

Serena and Chelsea sat side by side in the visitor's gallery to watch. The motion was introduced, and Chelsea's eyes moved around the House of Commons as, one by one, each minister stood up.

Are they taking attendance? she wondered. *Okay, good, everyone's here. Let's get started.*

Suddenly everyone was looking at them and clapping. Only then did she and Serena understand. Each MP had stood up to vote "yes," and it was unanimous. Every single minister had voted to pass the motion. It was a moment Serena and Chelsea would never forget. Although Shannen wasn't there to witness it, they both knew how much this fulfilment of her dream would have meant to her.

In March 2012 John Duncan, minister of the renamed Ministry of Aboriginal Affairs and Northern Development, announced that construction on a new school in Attawapiskat would begin. The building would be big enough for 540 students, from kindergarten to grade 8. After a vote in Attawapiskat, the long-awaited school was named Kattawapiskak, a traditional Cree name for the community.

And at last, in September 2014, excited students walked through the doors to start the school year in their brand-new school. It was a victory and a turning point for the whole community.

The fight for the school had lasted 10 years. "When they announced that we were going to get a new school, which was the fourth time," Chelsea Edwards said, "I wasn't sure if I should believe it. And the only way I would believe it was when I'd see the new school standing. And right now it is standing. And it's a dream come true."

"Every time I do step into that school," she added, "Shannen's memory will always come to mind."

> "I would tell the children not to be afraid . . . and follow their dreams. I would tell them NEVER give up hope."
>
> – Shannen Koostachin

Following in Shannen's Footsteps

Shannen Koostachin was just 13 years old when she helped to start the biggest youth-led movement for children's rights in Canadian history. Before her tragic death at the age of 15, she had already made a tremendous impact, and her actions inspired others to do the same.

Besides winning the new school for Attawapiskat, the students behind Shannen's Dream secured from the government a greater investment in education for First Nations children. They did it by shining a light on conditions that had long been overlooked and ignored. But the struggle continues. Although

A statue honoring Shannen was unveiled in 2015 in New Liskeard, Ontario. The bronze memorial, created by Tyler Fauvelle, depicts Shannen dancing in the traditional Cree regalia she loved.

the government increased its funding of First Nations schools in 2012, activists pointed out that the increase still fell short of what is really needed. Shannen's friends know they need to stay vigilant, and they are not backing down.

Serena Koostachin returned to Attawapiskat and became chief of the Youth Band Council. Family and friends in Attawapiskat continue to be inspired by Shannen and the words she wrote when she was 13:

"I would tell the children not to be afraid . . . and follow their dreams. I would tell them NEVER give up hope. Get up, pick up your books, and GO TO SCHOOL (just not in portables)."

Student protesters in Chile clash with police in 2011.

AFFORDABLE SCHOOLS

Education for All: Chile's Student Protests

SANTIAGO, CHILE, AUGUST 2011

She didn't see the armored cars speeding toward them till it was too late to flee. Holding their handmade signs, Camila Vallejo and the other students had just begun to sing when suddenly they were surrounded by military vehicles screeching to a halt. The 23-year-old geography student stopped mid-song.

Moments later, a cloud of tear gas was spreading rapidly, threatening to engulf the whole group.

That was when she spotted the water cannons mounted on two of the trucks. Before she could brace herself, a torrent of water hit her body.

All around her, people were knocked down and pushed along the pavement by the stream. Drenched and clenching her stinging eyes shut, Camila felt another burst of tear gas touch her wet skin. The reaction of water and chemical was intense. Her skin burned; she couldn't move. It was almost impossible to breathe.

She wanted to stay and carry on with the protest, but this was too much. She and her companions scrambled to their feet, turned, and ran from the *carabineros*, the Chilean police, who were jumping down from the armored trucks in riot gear.

In the hours that followed, there was chaos in the streets of Santiago. Hundreds of students were running down the streets, away from police; other masked youths were hurling stones at the officers. What had begun as a student protest march had degenerated into a riot. By the end of the afternoon, 250 people had been arrested and 25 officers had been injured by rocks and paint bombs.

Camila retreated to the student council office and used her phone to listen to reports of the mayhem outside. This wasn't what she had wanted at all.

For Camila and the other students protesting that day, the issue was an important one: affordable schools for all the people of Chile. There had been many marches and protests already, and they had been growing bigger all summer. Today she had called for students to gather peacefully in the Plaza Italia

Students protesting in a park flee from police tear gas.

public park and march together along Santiago's main street. But before they had even left the park, the police had cracked down. And to make it worse, the government was blaming her for inciting violence in the streets.

"We don't want violence," Camila later told the crowd as she stood outside the presidential palace. "Our fight is not versus the police or to destroy commercial shops. Our fight is to recover the right to education. On that we have been emphatic and clear."

If the government saw her as a troublemaker, others were calling Camila a folk hero. In either case, she was impossible to ignore. And she was not alone. Thousands of young people were on her side, with many older Chileans now joining in a fight that had been gaining momentum since May. What had started as a modest student campaign was now the biggest protest movement Chile had seen in over 20 years.

Sparking Change

While Camila Vallejo was growing up in Chile, her country was a democracy. But her parents remembered a different time. They had lived for 17 years under the brutal military dictatorship of General Augusto Pinochet. Camila's mother and father were both active in the resistance movement that stood up to Pinochet during the dictatorship. Luckily, neither was ever arrested. When Pinochet was forced to step down and Chile became a democracy in 1990, it was a huge victory for equal rights among Chileans.

"It is all about mine, mine, mine. There is not a lot of empathy for the other."

— Camila Vallejo, describing modern society in Chile

When Camila was a little girl, her father belonged to a political theater group that traveled around Chile. The troupe staged shows for miners about social injustice. Camila often went with him, excited to be part of it all. By the time she was a teenager, she wholeheartedly agreed with her parents' ideals.

At the time, Chile seemed prosperous, and it boasted some of the best schools in South America. Yet to Camila, it became obvious that there were two Chiles: one for the rich and one for the poor. For the few families who could afford it, there were a handful of elite private schools. The rest had to make do with underfunded, mediocre public schools.

And the cost of university in Chile, compared with the salary of the average Chilean, was the highest in the world. Getting a university degree meant borrowing money, and going deep into debt. It became clear to Camila that rich and middle-class families had access to some of the best schools in South America—at a very steep price—while working-class and poor students were left at an extreme disadvantage.

By the time she was in university herself, Camila was saddened and dismayed by the society she saw around her. She believed it had become selfish in its goals, and that for many all that mattered was money and personal success, rather than community. "It is all about mine, mine, mine," she once said. "There is not a lot of empathy for the other."

Camila was determined to help right some of the injustices in her country. While at the University of Chile, she decided to run for its student federation, a group that defended the rights of the students. It was there, she believed, that she could spark real change. And in the fall of 2010, Camila became the federation's new president. No one could have predicted then what a true force for change the band of students would become—and the powerful impact Camila would make as their leader.

"I began to understand that education could change people's lives"

Camila wasn't the only one fighting for change. At the same time, a young man named Giorgio Jackson was planting the seeds that would grow into a massive protest movement. Giorgio, an engineering student, was president of another student federation, at the Pontifical Catholic University of Chile. A thoughtful-looking young man with dark hair and a beard, the student president was usually seen around campus dressed casually in shorts and T-shirt.

Giorgio believed there was a basic problem with Chile's whole educational system: too many schools were motivated

Students Camila Vallejo (third from left) and Giorgio Jackson (far right) spearheaded the campaign for equal, affordable schools in Chile.

by making a profit, and students were treated as "customers." Meanwhile the government did little to guarantee quality in all schools. The richest students went to the best schools; the rest were shut out and forced to attend poorly funded, second-rate schools.

Like Camila, Giorgio was troubled by the growing gap between rich and poor in his country. He first tried to help by volunteering for a group that built houses for the homeless. "But there comes a time," he explained, "when you realize that volunteer work doesn't break the cycle of poverty." The answer, he suspected, lay elsewhere. "I began to understand," he said, "that education could change people's lives."

Children of Democracy: A Generation Takes Action

Giorgio began to talk to other students about campaigning for a fairer school system. He found an eager audience for his ideas. He could see a big difference between his parents' generation, which was grateful just to have thrown off a dictatorship, and his own age group. In Chile, people called them the "children of democracy." They expected more.

"We grew up in the absence of dictatorship, without a curfew and without seeing armed forces on the street," Giorgio described. "This made us freer. All of our lives we've been able to say what we think without being afraid of repression, and that's key when it comes to forming a social movement."

"All of our lives we've been able to say what we think without being afraid of repression, and that's key when it comes to forming a social movement."

– *Giorgio Jackson*

Giorgio knew that Chile's government was deeply opposed to change. If he wanted to make things happen, he would have to join forces with other student groups and federations—including Camila's. As Giorgio said, "It was David versus Goliath." United, perhaps the students had a chance.

Spreading the Word

Newly banded together, the student leaders decided their first step was to get their message out to all students throughout Chile. After much discussion and advice, they boiled it down to three key ideas.

> "There is more than enough money in Chile to make education free."
>
> — Giorgio Jackson

First, access to higher education was unequal. Giorgio realized this was the easiest to explain. Among Chile's poorest, only two out of ten people went to university. Among the richest, it was nine out of ten. And poor students were much more likely to drop out, unable to carry the financial burden to the end of school.

Second, the government was not contributing its fair share to paying for education. Yet Chile was rich in natural resources, such as copper. As Giorgio said, "There is more than enough money in Chile to make education free."

Third, the government was not regulating schools to make sure the teaching was of a high quality. Too many inferior universities were handing out worthless degrees that did not lead to jobs—all in the name of money making.

Giorgio Jackson wanted to get this information out; he wanted wealthy Chileans to feel guilty, and poor ones to get angry. The students created a webpage and produced a video to post online. Giorgio knew they were on to something when their video got 10,000 hits. Their ultimate goal was to rally students for a protest march in May 2011 in the capital, Santiago. Giorgio realized that when people take to the streets, it has to be big.

The march was intended to expose the unfairness of the whole education system. But at the same time, the student leaders decided to keep their demands specific and reasonable—that way, they were more likely to get practical, helpful results.

The country had been damaged by a severe earthquake in 2010, and many elementary and high schools needed repairs to make them safe again—and things as basic as chairs and glass in the windows. So they made a plea for those repairs. The student leaders also asked for a small subsidy to help struggling university students pay for their meals.

Taking It to the Streets

The campaign paid off. Giorgio was overjoyed when roughly 30,000 people came out for the march. This was a huge success! Encouraged, they planned another rally for later in the month—and this time, 40,000 marched through the streets of Santiago. "People were motivated," Giorgio said. "They felt like they were participating in something big."

Now the students waited anxiously to see what would happen next. Surely the government of President Sebastián Piñera

Camila and Giorgio help carry a sign during one of the massive rallies in Santiago, Chile's capital.

would have to take action in response to this impressive turn-out. The people had spoken. Would they win their demands?

But there was almost no response. Was the government planning to ignore the protesters, hoping they would go away? Well, if that was its strategy, it back-fired. University students who had never taken an interest in politics before were now alarmed. And many were angry at a government led by a "billionaire busi-nessman" who would not even meet a reasonable request for help in a crisis.

"Chile, you do everything for profit."

— graffiti in Santiago in August 2011

The protests continued and turned into occupations of whole streets, shut-ting down parts of the capital. The marchers now demanded what Giorgio called "the recovery of public education"—education as a right for all, not a privilege for the few. The movement spread be-yond Santiago, with marches and sit-ins happening in other cities, too.

The Face of the Movement

During these weeks, Camila Vallejo emerged as a vocal leader among the marching students. Giorgio Jackson had shown himself to be a thoughtful writer and planner, but Camila was charismatic and bold.

During the protest marches in Santiago, Camila walked at the head of the crowd, surrounded by her student "body-guards." She drew admirers, who shouted and waved to get her attention—most often high school boys who would call out, "Friend me on Facebook!"

Photos of Camila, with her long brown hair and nose ring, began to appear in the media alongside stories of the protests. Clearly she was becoming the "face" of the student movement. Soon she was invited to appear on TV talk shows to explain the students' cause. When Camila talked about the issues, they didn't sound complicated at all—it was all about fairness and common sense. And she was especially adept at using social media to spread the message. Within months she had hundreds of thousands following her Twitter posts, where she commented on the government or told people where and when to meet for upcoming protests.

Camila Vallejo leads the way on a protest march.

Passion for Education

As the student protests spread, the organizers became more inventive. Camila Vallejo organized *cacerolazos*—protests with marchers banging pots and pans, a traditional way of showing dissent. Students even held "superhero" protests, huge gatherings of youths dressed as Superman, Wonder Woman, and other favorite caped superheroes. Student couples staged a "kiss-in" in Santiago, where they smooched and held up signs that declared their "passion for education." Others staged giant pillow fights, or lay down in the streets, blocking roads. The more bizarre the protests, the more the media took notice, and soon the education protests in Chile were international news.

ONDENADOS X LA EDUCACIO

Protests get creative: students hold up "bars" to show they
are imprisoned by inferior education.

The protests often seemed like carnivals, full of smiling
students enjoying the excitement. But behind the circus antics,
the intention was serious.

Teens Take a Stand

Soon high school students were joining in with their own
protests. Chile's high school system was also divided between
expensive private schools and poorly funded public ones. By
June, hundreds of thousands of high school as well as university
students were refusing to go to class. Classes were canceled in
dozens of high schools around the country as teens camped out,
occupying sections of the buildings day and night. They arrived
carrying blankets and snacks—often packed by supportive
parents who were tired of the inequality and high costs of
schools. The students settled in for a long occupation.

"We're not fighting for ourselves, but for everyone else and our own future children," one 15-year-old boy said.

"Our dreams are no one's property!"

"We're not fighting for ourselves, but for everyone else and our own future children."

– *Chilean high school student*

In early July, President Piñera reacted—at last. He proposed a new government fund for higher education that would provide more student grants and loans to help pay tuition costs. He suggested that private universities might pay taxes that could be used for scholarships for poorer students. But for Giorgio Jackson, Camila Vallejo, and the other student leaders, it was no longer enough. Encouraged by the massive turnout for their protests, the student leaders had moved on to a more ambitious goal: high-quality public education that everyone could afford. The government must take control of the country's schools, both high schools and universities, funding them and making them equal.

Camila explained that making improvements to the existing system wasn't good enough. "We want a profound change . . . to see education as a right, where the state provides a guarantee."

In August the protest marches reached a peak: 500,000 people attended a protest organized by Giorgio and other student leaders in Santiago's O'Higgins Park. Giorgio spoke to the crowd, later describing the experience as "a moment I am never going to forget. The crowds and the energy created a sense that we were doing something of real significance. I'm proud to have been there."

Students defy police orders to stop marching, bearing a sign that reads, "Our ideals are not repressed."

The Police Crack Down

So far the student protests had been peaceful. Now events took a violent turn. At marches, youths hiding their faces under hoodies and scarves started throwing stones at police, smashing store windows, and inciting riots. Camila declared firmly that the rioters were from outside the student movement. They were not taking direction from her or any other leader; the student movement was nonviolent.

Nonetheless, in early August the government banned any more demonstrations. "The time for marching has run out," announced a government minister. The protests were now illegal and would be met with force.

"Education is not for profit; our dreams are no one's property!"

— popular slogan from the student protests

Despite the warning, defiant students rallied in Santiago's Plaza Italia for another march. Riot police moved in, using tear gas and water cannons to scatter the students. Some protesters set up barricades with burning tires, and scuffles followed between police and masked stone-throwers. Youths stood on rooftops shooting rocks from slingshots. Hundreds of students fled the scene, but many others were arrested.

"My whole body was burning. It was brutal."

– Camila Vallejo

Camila was there when the riot police descended. That was when she was hit with tear gas and doused with one of the water cannons. "My whole body was burning," she said. "It was brutal." Outraged, Camila later described the situation as a "state of siege."

Police use water cannons to disperse crowds of protesters.

Next came a crackdown on the high school students camped out in their schools. The mayor of Santiago issued an order to evict them once and for all. Police used water cannons to force out students occupying three high schools.

"The use of force was necessary for the rule of law," said the police chief.

But once again, Piñera's actions seemed to have the opposite effect to what he intended. When bedraggled students returned home with stories of being tear-gassed and soaked by water cannons, their parents were alarmed. Now more and more Chileans began to question the government's actions. Across the country, Piñera's approval rating sank to an all-time low.

Camila Vallejo knew that a single image could send a powerful message. She and her fellow students got busy gathering up the empty tear-gas canisters that police had used against the students, and they made them into an enormous peace sign. The picture appeared widely in newspapers around the world and online.

As the face of the student movement, Camila had enemies as well as fans. One government minister even suggested threateningly that the protests would end if someone got rid of Vallejo. That minister lost her job soon after. But Camila had reason to be nervous, and by the end of August, Chile's supreme court had ordered police protection for the student leader. When someone posted Camila's address online, her parents worried that she was in too much danger to stay at home, even with police watching. They persuaded her to move out for her own safety.

"We took the first step, but we are no longer alone"

"It is always the youth that make the first move."

– Camila Vallejo

At the peak of the protests that summer, 70 to 80 percent of Chileans agreed with the students' demand to make education affordable for all. "The youth now have more credibility than the traditional politicians," said one Santiago student. Other groups took to the streets as well, including striking transport workers and miners. Like a tumbling stone causing an avalanche, the student movement was turning into a general demand for better democracy in Chile. The students had given voice to something essential that had been troubling many Chileans.

"There are huge levels of discontent," said Camila. "It is always the youth that make the first move . . . we don't have family commitments, this allows us to be freer. We took the first step, but we are no longer alone, the older generations are now joining this fight."

Support for the students was growing internationally as well. A German folk rock group composed a tribute, while students in Mexico made a video about Camila and her cause. In December, a newspaper in England named her its "Person of the Year," while Spanish media depicted her as a glamorous Latin American revolutionary. In Brazil, student protesters invited her to come and march with them.

Camila valued this encouragement: "Here in Chile we are constantly hearing the message that our goals are impossible and that we are unrealistic, but the rest of the world, especially the youth, are sending us so much support."

The fight was far from over. Throughout 2012 the protests continued: more sit-ins at schools, further clashes with police. Despite the bans and the efforts of the riot police, the students were not backing down.

From Protester to Politician

In 2013, Camila Vallejo and Giorgio Jackson made a bold decision. They would run for election to Chile's government. Both believed that big reforms needed to happen in Chile and that they could better push for change from within the government. In addition to making education equal and available to all, the young leaders now wanted to push for a new constitution and fairer elections, and other policies to close the gap between rich and poor.

In the November 2013 elections, both Jackson and Vallejo won seats in Parliament. At 25, Vallejo was the youngest member of the new government. Two other student leaders were also elected. And the elections ushered in a new president, Michelle Bachelet. She promised to make education a top priority. By the end of her term in office, she said, the government would pay the tuition of the poorest 70 percent of higher-education students.

In her victory speech, Bachelet thanked the young protesters who had "set the country on its course." Bachelet's words sounded promising, but the student leaders knew they would have to watch and see if those words were put into action.

In 2014, the government took a big step forward with its proposed Education Reform Bill—which immediately became controversial. Student leaders demanded to be more involved, and protesters once more took to the streets—80,000 strong in

After their successful protest movement, Camila and Giorgio both ran for election to Chile's parliament.

Santiago. In November high school teachers and their students staged a 48-hour walkout, closing schools across the country, to protest the slow progress of reform as well as the exclusion of teachers from the debate.

A Debate that Rages On

The student campaign that began in 2011 snowballed into the biggest protest movement in Chile since the overthrow of its dictator and the return to democracy in 1990. Again and again, the students showed courage and resolve in the face of armed opposition and government attempts to repress protest. They also demonstrated the power of mass popular movements to push for political change.

As Giorgio Jackson noted, that change has not been perfect, but the protests have yielded encouraging results. A substantial increase in the number of poor students receiving government scholarships is one clear victory. But just as important, the protests finally opened up what Giorgio called a "healthy debate" about what the role of a school should be. Was the ideal of "free education for all" hopelessly unrealistic or a fundamental right? That debate rages on, but the fact that it is finally taking place is another victory.

According to Giorgio, not only did the students "move the debate forward," they turned a government that was resistant to change and deaf to protest into a one in which "different political forces dare to consider different options."

In Giorgio's words, "We have changed the realm of what is possible."

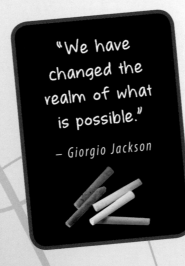

"We have changed the realm of what is possible."

— Giorgio Jackson

Afterword

In its Universal Declaration of Human Rights, the United Nations states that "everyone has the right to education." It also declares that elementary education "shall be free," and higher education "shall be equally accessible to all on the basis of merit." And yet today, millions of children worldwide are denied this basic right.

UNESCO has estimated that 59 million children of primary school age and nearly 65 million teenagers are not in school—that's 124 million children between the ages of 6 and 15 who are not getting an education. And for many more who do attend school, the education they get is inadequate: about 250 million children around the world cannot read, write, or do basic math.

The barriers between these children and their right to learn are multiple: poverty, child labor, war, and discrimination all play a role. In 2000, UNICEF and UNESCO started a global initiative to identify these vulnerable children, the barriers to their success, and the policy changes that would end their exclusion from schools. In the 15 years since, several countries have cut their number of out-of-school children by half, by investing in solutions such as free tuition, scholarships, and non-formal programs to reach the most marginalized children. Around the world, other local initiatives have also helped to break down the barriers. But the fight to learn is still in progress: much remains to be done before the UN's vision of education for all becomes a reality.

Main Sources

The Boy with a School in His Backyard

Chakrabarti, Samrat. "The little headmaster and his big homework."
    Tehelka Magazine, Vol. 6, Issue 47. Tehelka.com, 28 November 2009.
    Web.

Hassan, Tanvir. "Babar Ali—World's youngest headmaster making
    remarkable changes in India." *Youth Leader*. Youth Leader Magazine,
    n.d. Web.

"The 'youngest headmaster in the world.'" *BBC News*. BBC, 12 October
    2009. Web.

The Roma

"Breaking the cycle of exclusion for Roma in Romania." *The World Bank*.
    The World Bank Group, 7 April 2014. Web.

"Brief: Roma." *The World Bank*. The World Bank Group, 24 February
    2015. Web.

"Case Study: How one community was able to get every child in school."
    OvidiuRo. Asociatia OvidiuRo, July 2010. Web.

Edwards, Joelle. "A landmark en passant: Florence's English Cemetery
    Part II." *The Florentine*. The Florentine, 3 June 2010. Web.

Gillet, Kit. "Leslie Hawke helps Roma children get an education."
    Christian Science Monitor. The Christian Science Monitor, 10 January
    2014. Web.

Holloway, Julia Bolton. "Bicameral education, holistic education."
    "English" Cemetery and Its Library, Florence. Blogger, 8 December
    2014. Web.

Holloway, Julia Bolton. "Why I'd rather teach illiterate Roma than Princeton students." *Quartz*. Quartz, 29 November 2014. Web.

Le Bas, Damian. "Yes, Gypsies lag in education, but the reasons are complex and cultural." *The Guardian*. Guardian News and Media Ltd., 22 January 2014. Web.

Löfgren, Emma. "Sweden invests millions in ending Roma racism." *The Local: Sweden's News in English*. The Local Europe AB, 8 April 2015. Web.

"Marijana's story: From a poor Roma childhood to international social development expert." *The World Bank*. The World Bank Group, 8 April 2015. Web.

"Roma advocate scoops Wallenberg prize." *The Local: Sweden's News in English*. The Local Europe AB, 27 August 2014. Web.

Gender: Girls in the Muslim World

Ayed, Nahlah. "Malala's friends, also wounded, push for girls' education." *CBC News*. CBC/Radio-Canada, 8 October 2013. Web.

Baker, Aryn. "The other girls on the bus: How Malala's classmates are carrying on." *Time*. Time Inc., 19 December 2012. Web.

"Battle over girls' education in Pakistan's Swat Valley." *BBC News*. BBC, 3 May 2013. Web.

"Defying the Taliban to get an education." *BBC News*. BBC, 15 October 2009. Web.

"Malala's friend Shazia Ramzan moves to UK." *BBC News*. BBC, 2 July 2013. Web.

"Pakistan's education crisis." *Alif Ailaan*. Alifailaan.pk, 2015. Web.

Smallman, Etan. "The other Malalas: Shazia Ramzan and Kainat Riaz's incredible journey from Pakistan to Wales." *Independent*. The Independent, 3 January 2015. Web.

Taqdees, Maria. "Change agent inspires community." *YES Programs: Impact Stories*. Kennedy-Lugar Youth Exchange and Study Program, 26 May 2012. Web.

Taqdees, Maria. "YES Community Learning Center: Basic literacy to vocational skills." *YES Programs: Impact Stories*. Kennedy-Lugar Youth Exchange and Study Program, 26 January 2016. Web.

Outcasts from Learning: Teaching the Untouchables

Dutta, Ambarish. "The story of Cycle Sister." *Tribune India Online Edition.*
    The Tribune Trust, 12 February 2006. Web.
Nolen, Stephanie. "What's better than a miracle school for 'untouchable'
    girls?" *Globe and Mail.* The Globe and Mail Inc., 8 June 2012. Web.
Nolen, Stephanie. "You can unlock the potential of India's Dalit girls, but
    where can they use it?" *Globe and Mail.* The Globe and Mail Inc.,
    10 December 2011. Web.
Srivastava, Amitabh. "Marginalized girls find hope in Sudha." *IndiaToday.*
    India Today Group, 18 November 2008. Web.

Caught in the Crossfire

Glass, Ira. "Harper High School, part one." *This American Life, WBEZ.*
    Chicago Public Media, 15 February 2013. Web. Transcript.
Glass, Ira. "Harper High School, part two." *This American Life, WBEZ.*
    Chicago Public Media, 22 February 2013. Web. Transcript.
Hutson, Wendell. "Gates scholars inspire Englewood students." *DNAinfo
    Chicago.* DNAinfo.com, 26 April 2013. Web.
Hutson, Wendell. "Harper Students: White House visit 'once-in-a-lifetime
    experience'" *DNAinfo Chicago.* DNAinfo.com, 7 June 2013. Web.
Hutson, Wendell. "Mayor Rahm Emanuel puts $4.5 million in anti-violence
    programs for youth." *DNAinfo Chicago.* DNAinfo.com, 7 February
    2013. Web.
Lutton, Linda. "Harper High boasts two Gates Millennium Scholars, despite
    school's struggle with violence." *WBEZ.* Chicago Public Media,
    22 April 2013. Web.
Lutton, Linda. "The weight of the city's violence, on one school principal."
    WBEZ. Chicago Public Media, 9 July 2012. Web.
Slevin, Peter. "Chicago grapples with gun violence: Murder toll soars."
    Washington Post. The Washington Post, 21 December 2012. Web.
Smith, Mitch. "First Lady cites Chicago violence in CBS interview."
    Chicago Tribune. Chicagotribune.com, 6 May 2013. Web.

Forced into Battle

"About Hope North and Okello Sam." *Hope North*. Hope North USA, n.d. Web.

Beadle, Dixie. "Okello Kelo Sam: Artist and activist," in *Men of the Global South: A Reader*. Ed. Adam Jones. New York: Zed Books, 2006.

"Child Soldier." *War Child*. War Child UK, 2014. Web.

Kelly, Linda. "Once a child soldier, now a provider of hope." *Fellowship Magazine*, vol. 77, no. 4-6. Fellowship of Reconciliation, 2012. Web.

"The Lord's Resistance Army." *War Child*. War Child UK, 2014. Web.

Shannen Koostachin: The Right to a "Real School"

Angus, Charlie. *Shannen and Serina Koostachin Nov. 2009*. YouTube, 16 October 2012. Web.

Angus, Charlie. "Shannen Koostachin 'really believed that kids could change the world.'" *Huffington Post*. TheHuffingtonPost.com, Inc., 1 October 2012. Web.

Goyette, Linda. "Still waiting in Attawapiskat." *Canadian Geographic Magazine*. Canadian Geographic Enterprises, December 2010. Web.

Hi-Ho Mistahey! Dir. Alanis Obomsawin. National Film Board of Canada, 2013. NFB.ca. Web.

Koostachin, Shannen. "Shannen's letter to the Committee for the International Peace Prize." *Shannen's Dream*. First Nations Child and Family Caring Society of Canada, n.d. Web.

Shannen's Dream. Dir. Shelley Steele. Heartspeak Productions, 2011. DVD.

Education for All: Chile's Student Protests

"Chile police break up student protest in Santiago." *BBC News*. BBC, 4 August 2011. Web.

Forero, Juan. "Education protests shake Chile's government." *Washington Post*. The Washington Post, 18 August 2011. Web.

Franklin, Jonathan. "Camila Vallejo—Latin America's 23-year-old new revolutionary folk hero." *Guardian*. Guardian News and Media Ltd., 8 October 2011. Web.

Goldman, Francisco. "Camila Vallejo, the world's most glamorous revolutionary." *New York Times*. The New York Times Company, 5 April 2012. Web.

Jackson, Giorgio. "Students of change: How a call for education access became a cry for true democracy," in *From Cairo to Wall Street: Voices from the Global Spring*. Ed. Anya Schiffrin and Eamon Kircher-Allen. New York: The New Press, 2012.

Long, Gideon. "Chile's student leaders come of age." *BBC News*. BBC, 11 March 2014. Web.

Long, Gideon. "Chile student protests point to deep discontent." *BBC News*. BBC, 11 August 2011. Web.

Education Statistics

"Data Centre: Country profiles." *UNESCO*. UNESCO Institute for Statistics, 2014. Web.

"Out-of-school numbers rise as aid to education falls short of 2010 levels." *All in School: The Global Initiative on Out-of-School Children*. UNESCO Institute of Statistics, 6 July 2015. Web.

Further Reading

Duckworth, Katie. *Children's Rights: Education*. London: Save the Children with Evans Brothers Ltd., 2004.

Hughes, Susan. *Off to Class: Incredible and Unusual Schools around the World*. Toronto: Owlkids, 2011.

Humphreys, Jessica Dee, and Michel Chikwanine. *Child Soldier: When Boys and Girls Are Used in War*. Toronto: Kids Can Press, 2015.

Kyuchukov, Hristo, and Ian Hancock. *A History of the Romani People*. Honesdale, Pa.: Boyds Mills Press, 2005.

Smith, Penny. *A School Like Mine: A Unique Celebration of Schools around the World*. New York, Dorling Kindersley, 2007.

Wilson, Janet. *Shannen and the Dream for a School*. Toronto: Second Story Press, 2011.

Yousafzai, Malala, with Patricia McCormick. *I Am Malala: How One Girl Stood up for Education and Changed the World (Young Readers Edition)*. New York: Little, Brown and Co., 2014.

Index

Image Credits

Acknowledgements

Many thanks to everyone who helped to shape the ideas in this book, especially Rivka Cranley at Annick Press and editor Catherine Marjoribanks.